STUDY GUIDE

LOOKING UP

 All emphasis within Scripture quotations is the author's own. Please note that Destiny Image's publishing style capitalizes certain pronouns that refer to the Father, Son, and Holy Spirit, and may differ from some publishers' styles. Take note that the name satan and related names are not capitalized. We choose not to acknowledge him, even to the point of violating grammatical rules.

DESTINY IMAGE® PUBLISHERS, INC.
P.O. Box 310, Shippensburg, PA 17257-0310
"Promoting Inspired Lives."

This book and all other Destiny Image and Destiny Image Fiction books are available at Christian bookstores and distributors worldwide.

For more information on international distributors, call 717-532-3040.
Reach us on the Internet: www.destinyimage.com.

ISBN 13 TP: 978-0-7684-7200-4
ISBN 13 eBook: 978-0-7684-7201-1

For Worldwide Distribution, Printed in the U.S.A.
1 2 3 4 5 6 7 8 / 27 26 25 24 23

STUDY GUIDE

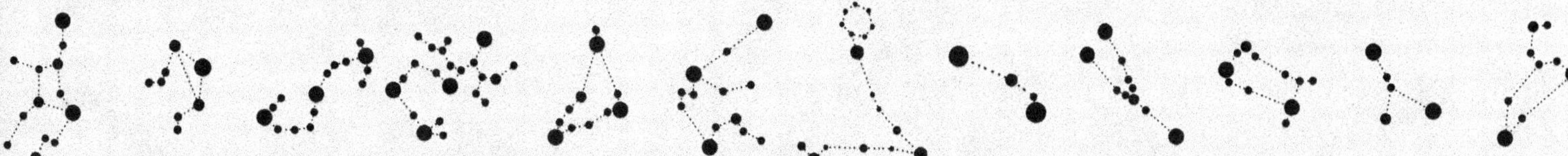

LOOKING UP

BOOK ONE

PROPHETIC SIGNS IN THE CONSTELLATIONS AND HOW THE HEAVENS DECLARE THE GLORY OF GOD

TROY A BREWER

CONTENTS

Welcome to *Looking Up!*

Hi! I'm Troy Brewer, the author of *Looking Up,* the book you are about to study. I'm your guide for the adventure with God you are about to experience. But realize here at the beginning that you will not see or hear what God wants you to see and hear unless He reveals it to you. You can collect a lot of facts and ideas about the stars in this study, but God wants you to have a revelation of *who He is* in the weeks to come!

As I always say, you'll need your Bible open during this study! And yet this study is also about what God said before His Spirit spoke and inspired the Bible we read. You see, before God's message was recorded in the Bible, it was written in the heavens. God's handwritten Word goes back to Moses and Job; God's star-written Word was published in the first week of creation.

Think about the giant marquee in Times Square that shows a constant parade of words in lights moving across the screen with their message. Now imagine that the message is moving from right to left instead of left to right. The language of two-thirds of God's Word is Hebrew, written from right to left, so it's no surprise that He would write in the heavens from right to left. The revolving story of God's plan for humanity cycles counter-clockwise in the stars, proclaiming God's message since He spoke them into existence on the fourth day of creation.

The stars that first grabbed my attention as a boy continue to speak to me half a century later. Whether this is your introduction to stargazing or you have been looking up for a long time, welcome to God's story written in lights. The more you see the way God has declared His glory in the heavens, the more you will want Him to open your eyes, your mind, and your heart to see and hear more.

Keep *Looking Up!*

TROY BREWER

LOOKING UP

LOOKING UP

LOOKING UP

LOOKING UP

Leader and User Guides (Read This First)

This study guide serves a dual purpose: as a guide for individuals who are eager to discover what God's Word tells us about the heavens and as suggested sessions for small group leaders and participants with questions and insights that will help them apply the Scriptures and content of the book *Looking Up*.

The sessions are based on chapters or sections of chapters. Whether you are studying alone or in a small group, as you read the assigned pages, take a moment to jot your thoughts and questions immediately after your reading. These will help you as you work on the lesson on your own or with others.

[NOTE: Leader Notes will be enclosed in brackets]

[Make sure to secure a copy of the book *Looking Up*, Looking Up Prophetic Pictures in the Heavens Map, and a copy of this study guide for each group member. KEY: Encourage everyone to read the first book assignment (pages 19-24 of Chapter One) before the first session. You may even want to have a preliminary session to pass out the materials and let the group meet one another.]

This study guide has three parts: Front Matter (what you're reading now), Study Sessions (the discussion guides), and Leader/Group Helps (tools to make this and further small group studies great for you).

Each session will include enough material to gather for one to two hours. There is also a daily follow-up alongside the reading of the next assignment in *Looking Up*. Decide as a group how long you want the sessions to be and handle the content that way.

Note throughout this study guide that I've written the quoted Scripture verses in BOLD so that we are all clear when God is speaking to us.

[Spend some time on YouTube watching Pastor Brewer's four Star Party videos, becoming familiar with the language of the stars viewed from God's Word and a prophetic outlook. KEY IDEA: You might even plan a star party in which you binge-watch those YouTube videos with your group—they take about 30 minutes each. You can also purchase his *Looking Up* 2-Conference DVD or Digital Download from TroyBrewer.com. It is a great resource!]

[Find out if there are any planetariums in your area or other sources of information on the heavens. You might want to plan a "road trip to the stars" for your group.]

[Be sure to check out the Leader/Group Helps section for lots of resources and suggestions from others who have been down the same road of leadership.]

Overview of the Looking Up Prophetic Pictures in the Heavens Map

This two-sided fold-up "map" is a treasure trove of visual insights into the heavens and the firmament. It's a beautiful example of ways the *"heavens declare the glory of God and the firmament shows His handiwork"* (Psalm 19:1). As Pastor Troy explains the two terms in this key verse, *heavens* is the wide, general scope of creation, the vast reaches of space; *firmament* is made up of the unchanging, regular, repeating, sure aspects of God's creation. It is literally our view of the universe from planet Earth because God created the universe to be seen from our perspective. He is speaking to us and only us through these signs in the heavens!

As you open the map, you will notice one side is mostly blue—this is the heavens side, and it represents the scope of prophetic pictures God has placed in our view. Some of these are events (like eclipses) and some of them are apparently random objects (like comets)—though comets are regular on a larger scale than daily, monthly, yearly as the signs in the firmament are.

The right section of the blue side of the map is part of the larger red side, which unpacks the firmament—unchanging, regular, predictable, aspects of the creation that mirror our unchanging God. The section called Prophetic Pictures in the Heavenly Signs begins on the blue side and takes up most of the red side—this is a brief guide to each of the 12 signs in the heavens, beginning with Virgo and ending with Leo. Each listing includes a key Scripture passage, a prophetic word related to that sign's message, and an explanation of the numeric aspects of that sign's placement. There is also an Overview of the signs and their message which you should seek to memorize, as it captures the essence of God's grand story of salvation written in the stars.

Take note of the Prophetic Words in Planets section (on the blue side), which introduces the kinds of prophetic or "supernatural" insights that are reflected in our solar system. One example is the Prophetic Pictures and the 12 Tribes of Israel, which lays out the parallel between the identities of the sons/tribes of Jacob and the constellations in God's firmament story.

This Prophetic Pictures in the Heavens Map will help you throughout the study and beyond to review what you are learning. When you are finished, you will see the big picture of all God is declaring in the heavens and the firmament.

Outline for Each Session

The following notes give you a sense of the flow and components of each of the sessions.

> [Leaders should note the approximate time allotted for each part of the session, so you can keep on track with the agreed length of the sessions.]

Title

The session titles reflect the chapter sections in the *Looking Up* book, highlighting the prophetic reading of the stars and constellations alongside God's Word that underlies this teaching.

Memory Verse

A Bible verse will be suggested for memorization/meditation in each session. It will relate to the main theme of the study for that week.

> [Encourage members of the group to memorize and offer opportunities for them to recite individually or as a group. Point out times when the MEMORY VERSE comes up in discussion.]

Looking Up Reading Assignment for This Week

Not only will there be reading assignments in the book, the Prophetic Pictures in the Heavens Map will also be highlighted in each session. Both tools should be used as part of preparation for the group sessions or to supplement your individual study.

Preparing and Discussing

A brief opening thought will set the stage for the themes and content of each session. It may include highlights from the assigned reading in *Looking Up*.

Looking Up

This section will include some warm-up questions to help the group focus on the theme for the session and perhaps review a previous discussion.

[Use some or all of these questions depending on the level of interaction by the group. Also included will be some group activities and "housekeeping" suggestions involving hosting duties, prayer requests, group contact information, etc.]

The Word and the Message of the Stars

This section will introduce one or more key Bible passages related to the theme and will explore the group's understanding of the content in the book reading assignment.

Here you will find some space for your own notes and perhaps some clarifying notes that may help in the discussion.

[The questions will review the reading assignment, focus on clarifying the biblical passages, and emphasize observation: What do these readings **say**? Those who complete the questions included at the end of the chapter will be more prepared to interact during the group sessions.]

Study Notes

When needed or helpful, this section will offer some additional insights from the Scripture passages being used that may be helpful during the discussion or for further study.

[Review these in preparing to lead the discussion. The notes may answer some questions that come up in the group.]

Looking Up and Seeing

Several questions will focus on the wider significance and principles related to the content of the biblical and book readings. What do these readings *mean*?

[Here the objective is for the group to work toward a clear grasp of the biblical truth or truths found in the study readings and how these truths relate to daily living.]

Applying the Word in the Constellations

The underlying point of gathering and studying God's Word together is the practical question of personal action. When we learn, the lesson will soon fade and be forgotten if we don't apply it to our lives. Here we will discuss specific actions we may undertake as a result of what we've discussed in the session.

[Here the purpose will be to help group members engage personally with the challenges found in the book. How does understanding God's Word and His call to me affect my life?]

Final Matters

This section will include reminders to share prayer requests.

It will also offer a closing thought from Pastor Troy as the group ends the session.

Looking Up Reading Assignment for Next Week

This is where the fun begins. Join Pastor Troy as he debunks the lie of the Zodiac and unveils the true story in the stars—or the Mazzaroth—Heaven's Bible.

Daily Follow-Up

Here you will find five follow-up Scripture readings with a brief devotional question to encourage journaling and prayer between sessions.

[Encourage your group members to use these and consider including the daily questions in your discussions during the sessions.]

Session One

Eyes to See and Ears to Hear

Memory Verse

Lift up your eyes on high, and see who has created these things, Who brings out their host by number; He calls them all by name. By the greatness of His might and the strength of His power; not one is missing.

—ISAIAH 40:26

It happens all the time: we look, but don't see; we listen, but don't hear. God know this. That's why the Word implores us to have eyes to see and ears to hear! How many times have you lost your keys or glasses only to find them right in the spot you already looked? How often has your spouse or parent had to repeat things three times before you said, "What did you say?" God has the same problem with us, and He demonstrates His grace and love by showing and telling us things over and over again. One thing we can never say to God is, "You didn't show me; You didn't tell me." Romans 1:20 makes it clear: we are "without excuse" when it comes to seeing and hearing God. Pray during this study that God's Spirit will powerfully improve your eyesight and hearing to what He has waiting for you when you Look Up.

Looking Up Reading Assignment for This Session

The first half of Chapter One (pages 19-24). Familiarize yourself with the Looking Up Prophetic Pictures in the Heavens Map.

Preparing and Discussing

Questions to help you engage with the themes for the session.

> [If the group is new and doesn't know one another, make sure you have name tags or take time to have each person introduce themselves briefly.]
>
> [The questions will always be written as if you are asking them. Consider assigning a member each time to ask the questions. Feel free to use only

some of the questions or alter the wording to fit your style or the group's. Encourage the group members to bring their Bible, Prophetic Pictures in the Heavens Map and their copy of the study guide to each session.]

1. As we begin this new study, what experiences have you had in stargazing? Describe where you would put yourself on the following continuum:

   Amateur 1 2 3 4 5 6 7 8 9 10 "I have my own well-worn telescope."

2. How would you say that looking at the stars naturally (astronomy) is different from astrology?

   Why do Christians believe astrology is a dangerous practice?

   Why do you think the Greek Zodiac is so different from the Hebrew Mazzaroth?

   Does God have the right to reclaim and redeem what sin and satan have distorted? How or why?

3. As you have studied and meditated on this session's memory verse (Isaiah 40:26), what thoughts and pictures has the Holy Spirit brought to mind?

The Word and the Message of the Stars

The following Bible passages are central to the opening chapter of *Looking Up*. Let's hear it read as we follow along, and we will include these verses in our conversation about the book.

PSALM 19:1-3

The heavens declare the glory of God; and the firmament shows His handiwork. Day unto day utters speech, and night unto night reveals knowledge. There is no speech nor language where their voice is not heard.

ROMANS 1:18-20

For the wrath of God is revealed from heaven against all ungodliness and unrighteousness of men, who suppress the truth in unrighteousness, because what may be known of God is manifest in them, for God has shown it to them.

For since the creation of the world His invisible attributes are clearly seen, being understood by the things that are made, even His eternal power and Godhead, so that they are without excuse.

2 TIMOTHY 3:16

All Scripture is given by inspiration of God, and is profitable for doctrine, for reproof, for correction, for instruction in righteousness.

2 CORINTHIANS 3:3

Clearly you are an epistle of Christ, ministered by us, written not with ink but by the Spirit of the living God, not on tablets of stone but on tablets of flesh, that is, of the heart.

4. If God's Word tells us (Psalm 19:1-3) that all of creation is declaring the glory of God, what are we doing when we fail to notice God's message in what He made?

Why do you think it is important to understand God's "Bible in the Heavens"?

Where do you most see (or hear) God's glory and handiwork in creation?

What is your personal fascination with the stars?

5. According to Pastor Troy, why did God put His plan for all humanity in the stars (page 20)?

Who qualifies to understand the plan?

6. Look up 2 Timothy 3:16. How can we apply this verse to our study of the stars?

What is the importance of rightly hearing what God is saying in the stars?

In His written Word?

7. According to Pastor Troy, what are the three ways the delivery of the Word of God works (pages 22-24)?

What differences do you find among the three?

How does the story of Jesus in the stars correspond with Paul's words to the Corinthians, *"written not with ink but by the Spirit of the living God, not on tablets of stone but on tablets of flesh, that is, of the heart"* (2 Corinthians 3:3)?

How is Paul's above statement about believers in the New Testament a fulfillment of Jeremiah 31:33 in the Old Testament?

8. Read the memory verse for this lesson found in Isaiah 40:26. How do the passages we just looked at make this verse even more significant to you?

Study Notes

The Bible gives us a reliable tool for seeing, hearing, and interpreting the signs and message of the stars. It gives us a great advantage over the ancients. But recognizing the accuracy, beauty, and original faithfulness of God's Word in creation should also humble us and drive us to worship. When we turn away from the stars and other aspects of creation as statements about God, we are missing out on God's glory.

Looking Up and Seeing

Let's explore together the meaning of some of what we've just been discovering.

9. Since God is the ultimate communicator, He certainly understands and uses non-verbal communication. What are some examples that demonstrate God "speaking loudly" without using words? (Example: In what ways is the cross of Jesus Christ the loudest non-verbal shout in history?)

   ______

   ______

   ______

   In your own words, what is the difference between God speaking in the natural and Him speaking in the supernatural or "prophetic"?

   ______

   ______

   ______

10. Compare and contrast the clarity of God's message in the stars versus Jesus' message in the parables (see pages 21-22).

    ______

    ______

    ______

How does Pastor Troy explain this?

11. Though the word *Zodiac* does not appear in the Bible, what ancient Hebrew word found in Job 38:32 and 2 Kings 23:5 is the older term for the same set of signs?

In practical application, how do you think the two are different?

How has the revelation of the Mazzaroth in the Bible changed your perception of the Signs in the Heavens known as the Zodiac?

12. What does Pastor Troy mean when he states that "Before it was written in the Bible, it was written in the heavens"? (See page 22.)

How does this "Bible in the Heavens" support Romans 1:20 which states, *"For since the creation of the world His invisible attributes are clearly seen, being understood by the things that are made, even His eternal power and Godhead, so that they are without excuse"*?

Do you see this as a positive or negative? Why?

Applying the Word in the Constellations

Let's get personal about the content of this chapter and the passages from God's Word we have been considering.

13. Let's open up our copies of the Looking Up Prophetic Pictures in the Heavens Map. We will refer to this often in our study. What is your first impression of all the information packed into these two big pages? How do you think it will be helpful as you seek to *Look Up?*

14. In what ways could seeing and hearing God's revelation to you in the heavenly signs in the night sky give you a greater sense of His immediate direction in your life?

Final Matters

A parting thought from Pastor Troy:

God is speaking. One of the endless number of His voices is the signs in the heavens, which is not without warning in scripture. God tells us worshipping the stars through horoscopes and assigning power and authority to them, not Him, brings fear and dismay. What is dismay? Dismay is alarm, shock, surprise, consternation, concern, distress, to be terrified. We are so small and the heavens are so vast. It's easy to see how so many civilizations looked at the stars as god instead of looking for the God who created the stars.

DEUTERONOMY 4:19

And take heed, lest you lift your eyes to heaven, and when you see the sun, the moon, and the stars, all the host of heaven, you feel driven to worship them and serve them, which the Lord your God has given to all the peoples under the whole heaven as a heritage.

JEREMIAH 10:1-2

Hear the word which the Lord speaks to you, O house of Israel. Thus says the Lord: "Do not learn the way of the Gentiles; do not be dismayed at the signs of heaven, for the Gentiles are dismayed at them."

The Bible warns of those who replace God with His creation. One definition of witchcraft is worshipping the created, not the creator. These people are astrologers—viewers of the heavens; and they are monthly prognosticators—those giving knowledge for heavenly events that can be predicted because they are part of a pattern.

2 KINGS 17:16

So they left all the commandments of the Lord their God, made for themselves a molded image and two calves, made a wooden image and worshiped all the host of heaven, and served Baal.

ISAIAH 47:13

You are wearied in the multitude of your counsels; let now the astrologers, the stargazers, and the monthly prognosticators stand up and save you from what shall come upon you.

Do not fear this study! The stars and God's true, authentic story in the signs rotating over our heads have never been a taboo subject in the Kingdom. Though the body of Christ has been driven away from this prophetic revelation by denominations, church boards and Christians who fear the Zodiac, they mistakenly try to "save" other Christians from the heart of Jesus Himself. This study will prove the heart of God displayed in the heavens is nothing to fear. My friend, you are just going to have to get past the witch hunters and really go after God's heart if you are going to let this revelation of the "Bible above us" impact you.

[As the session winds down, encourage the group to prepare for the next session and be in prayer for each of the other group members.]

Here are some last-minute tasks as we conclude this session:

Who can you invite to join you in this adventure pursuing this amazing revelation? [Discuss who might be good additions to the group.]

- *Looking Up* reading assignment for next week: Chapter One, (pages 24-48). Continue to review and familiarize yourself with the Looking Up Prophetic Pictures in the Heavens Map.

- Prayer requests from the group.

Close in prayer.

Daily Follow-Up

Day 1

Read: Genesis 1:14

Then God said, "Let there be lights in the firmament of the heavens to divide the day from the night; and let them be for signs and seasons, and for days and years...."

Respond: According to this verse, God established the lights in the firmament of the heavens with five purposes in mind. What are they?

How many of these are time oriented?

How many are message oriented?

What do you think the difference is between the two?

Day 2

Read: Isaiah 40:26

Lift up your eyes on high, and see who has created these things, Who brings out their host by number; He calls them all by name. By the greatness of His might and the strength of His power; not one is missing.

Respond: In this memory verse, how certain is the outlook for the world and the universe? Why?

If each star has a unique name and purpose that God gave it, what does that tell you about your identity and purpose?

Day 3

Read Matthew 2:1-2

Now after Jesus was born in Bethlehem of Judea in the days of Herod the king, behold, wise men from the East came to Jerusalem, saying, "Where is He who has been born King of the Jews? For we have seen His star in the East and have come to worship Him."

Respond: Why do you think God used a star to communicate the birth of Jesus to the world?

Did you know that God chose Daniel, a Jewish boy held captive in Babylon for 70 years, to teach the "magi" or the king's magicians, astrologers, and "wise men" to look for the birth of the Jewish messiah? He did. Why do you think God would use these pagan "wise men" to officially acknowledge the birth of Jesus?

Day 4

Read: Psalm 19:1

The heavens declare the glory of God; and the firmament shows His handiwork.

Respond: This really is the theme verse for the entire study. How do the heavens declare or speak of God's greatness to you?

Explain what *firmament* means and how it differs from what you thought this word meant before this revelation.

Day 5

Read: Psalm 19:2-3

Day unto day utters speech, and night unto night reveals knowledge. There is no speech nor language where their voice is not heard.

Respond: In your opinion, how do the stars speak to mankind as a whole?

How do they speak or "utter knowledge" to you, personally?

What does this verse mean by *"there is no speech or language where their voice is not heard"*?

Day 6

Use the following space to write any thoughts God has put in your heart and mind about the things we have looked at in this session and during your Daily Follow-Up time this week. If you haven't done so already, make sure to read the assignment for the next session in *Looking Up*.

Session Two

Prophetic, Visual, and Progressive

Memory Verse

Then God said, "Let there be lights in the firmament of the heavens to divide the day from the night; and let them be for signs and seasons, and for days and years...."

—GENESIS 1:14

Light showed up on the first day of creation and returned in a more specific way on the fourth day of God's grand masterpiece. God created light; then He created lights! He created night and day before He created the objects that divide day from the night. And instead of leaving us completely in the dark when night comes, God used the darkness as a backdrop to display His cosmic fireworks and light show. Every night, God provides a return engagement of the greatest show in the universe.

Looking Up reading assignment for this session:

- Chapter One (pages 24-48). Continue to review and familiarize yourself with the Looking Up Prophetic Pictures in the Heavens Map.

Preparing and Discussing

1. Let's have a quick report from everyone: in what ways have you been looking up and thinking differently about the stars since the last time we met?

___

___

___

2. As you have gotten more familiar with the Looking Up Prophetic Pictures in the Heavens Map, what things have you noticed that have been helpful to your thoughts on the Bible and God Himself?

___

___

___

Do you know the name of a specific star or constellation and why that name is significant to you?

3. Before starting this study, were you apprehensive about looking into the signs in the heavens? Why?

After reading the section "The Zodiac: The Greatest Deception of our Time" where Pastor Troy explains the difference between the revelation of the Mazzaroth and the Zodiac, how has the Gospel in the Heavens been hijacked to lead man away from God's plan? Why are horoscopes and Zodiac readings dangerous?

Throughout this section on deception, Pastor Troy shows the downward progression of idolatry and turning to the stars for guidance. What is that progression?

What is the proper place of the stars, constellations, signs in the heavens and Jesus' story in the stars within our lives?

The Word and the Message of the Stars

The following Bible passages connect with the main themes of the assignment in *Looking Up*. Let's hear them read as we follow along, and we will include these verses in our conversation about the book.

PSALM 8:3-5

When I consider Your heavens, the work of Your fingers, the moon and the stars, which You have ordained, what is man that You are mindful of him, and the son of man that You visit him? For You have made him a little lower than the angels, and You have crowned him with glory and honor.

PROVERBS 25:2

It is the glory of God to conceal a matter, but the glory of kings is to search out a matter.

MATTHEW 5:18

For assuredly, I say to you, till heaven and earth pass away, one jot or one tittle will by no means pass from the law till all is fulfilled.

4. One big difference between the Greek Zodiac and the Mazzaroth in the Bible is the place the story begins (pages 36-37). What is the starting point in the Zodiac story? What is the starting point in the Hebrew Mazzaroth?

____

____

What is so important about knowing the starting and ending points of this story?

____

____

____

What earthly structure testifies that the Mazzaroth tells the true story of God, creation and the universe?

5. In what sense are we the "kings" that Proverbs 25:2 talks about?

What does it mean to "search out a matter"?

What does it mean that God's story in the stars is prophetic?

What "tools" does God use to prophctically speak through the signs in the heavens?

How has the Prophetic Pictures in the Heavens Map helped you research what God is speaking through the heavens?

6. Jesus and the people of His day used the word *law* to refer to all of God's Word. How do the words from Jesus in Matthew 5:18 also speak of the heavens as part of God's Word?

Using your Prophetic Pictures in the Heavens Map, what is the definition of a sign?

How does it differ from a constellation?

Why do you think God uses signs to tell the major themes of His story?

How do the constellations support the narrative in the signs?

7. Commenting on Matthew 5:18, Pastor Troy notes, "Just like that, not only does the message of the constellations and stars prophesy Jesus our Redeemer, but even how they are placed from our perspective." The stars

are laid out and the constellations align from our point of view. What word does the Bible use to illustrate this?

Pastor Troy gives four examples of firmament (pages 40-45) and how they are unique to our view from earth. List and define each one in your own words.

Of these four examples of firmament, which blows your mind the most and why?

God created a universe with us as the audience in mind. What does this tell you about God's character? Of His view of you?

Study Notes

Pastor Troy points out that Earth is very likely the only planet in the universe that experiences a total eclipse. The sun and the moon, though of vastly different sizes and far from one another, appear from our point of view to be the same size. This means that when they perfectly align from time to time, the moon "blots out" the sun for a brief period—from our perspective. Colossians 1:15-16 tells us about Jesus,

> ***He is the image of the invisible God, the firstborn over all creation. For by Him all things were created that are in heaven and that are on earth, visible and invisible, whether thrones or dominions or principalities or powers. All things were created through Him and for Him.***

Apparently, while King Jesus was crafting the world and the surrounding universe, He thought it would be interesting to have a sun to give us light and heat along with an occasional "flicker" through eclipses to speak a great big message on the times we are living in (see Pastor Troy's "welcome" message and the "Prophetic Pictures in the Heavens" portion of your Prophetic Pictures in the Heavens Map).

Looking Up and Seeing

Let's explore the meaning of some of what we've just been studying.

8. In discussing how the "book of the heavens" works, Pastor Troy pointed to three big characteristics to keep in mind when reading the stars: their message is prophetic, visual, and progressive (or rotational/cyclical). From your reading and reflecting on the material, how would you explain each of these aspects of God's star book?

____

____

____

____

9. Why did the Dead Sea Scrolls have such an impact in demonstrating the unchanging nature of the written Word of God?

____

____

____

How does the unchanging, repeating nature of the pictures in the signs and constellations speak about the unchanging nature of God (pages 31-32)?

10. On pages 32-35, Pastor Troy offers a tutorial on the number 12 as it represents a consistent pattern God uses in getting our attention. What does the number 12 say about God?

    What does it say about His creation?

    Give an example that comes to your mind of 12 in the world or universe around you.

11. Looking closer at Polaris, the North Star, what message is God sending through its location in the heavens from our firmament?

In your own words, how can Jesus be seen in Polaris?

Where are you in this part of the story?

How has this one revelation of God's prophetic voice in creation changed the way you look up?

Applying the Word in the Constellations

Let's get personal about the content of these chapters and the passages from God's Word we have been studying.

12. If you've had exposure or even been taken in by the demonic errors and distortions in astrology, how is this study helping you turn away from that lie?

How are you beginning to see the true story of God written in the heavens?

In what ways are you eager to take ownership of this revelation to change your thinking, habits or life?

13. Pages 45-47 lay out the three stages of the cyclical/progressive message God repeats year in and year out in the heavens. We will travel through the sequence numerous times in this study. But for now, look at the basic connect-the-stars pictures and explain your personal observations. Which figures seem really clear to you? How does God's salvation story speak into your life right now?

Final Matters

A parting thought from Pastor Troy:

Just like the mobile over a baby's crib, space has always captured the human imagination. That's the point. King Jesus created the stars, planets, and heavens above to grab our attention and arouse our curiosity. They speak to us, don't they? Yes, the Word is the master communicator who spoke every star, planet, solar system and galaxy into just the right place to tell a story–His story–to generations and generations of people right here on what the Bible calls "the firmament." This, my friend, is where the revelation truly begins.

Think about it. Our solar system has been uniquely and carefully placed to give us a vantage point to see "out" of our galaxy and observe the universe with a breathtakingly clear view of other galaxies and amazing phenomena. The Word who later became flesh and dwelt among us created the universe to be seen and understood from our perspective. While incredible in itself, it is also deeply personal. Why would God Almighty care how we view the cosmos? Because He wants us to see Him in it and hear His voice. He wants us to see His hand of goodness at work. He is speaking a great big story of love, loss, and redemption for those curious enough to wonder, *Where do I fit in among all this grand design?*

[As the session winds down, encourage the group to prepare for the next session and be in prayer for each of the other group members.]

Here are some last-minute tasks as we conclude this session:

- *Looking Up* reading assignment for next week: Chapter Two (pages 50-71).
- Prayer requests from the group.

Close in prayer.

Daily Follow-Up

Day 1

Read: Psalm 8:3-5

When I consider Your heavens, the work of Your fingers, the moon and the stars, which you have ordained, what is man that You are mindful of him, and the son of man that You visit him? For You have made him a little lower than the angels, and You have crowned him with glory and honor.

Respond: We were made to look up at the heavens. When you look at the stars, what is God causing you to think about yourself?

Why do you think the stars and planets are such a fascination with mankind in general?

Day 2

Read: Genesis 1:14

Then God said, "Let there be lights in the firmament of the heavens to divide the day from the night; and let them be for signs and seasons, and for days and years…."

Respond: According to our definition of *firmament* as the universe from man's perspective on earth, what do the signs, seasons, days, and years all have in common?

Why would God want to divide day from night?

What is the supernatural (prophetic) picture of the natural phenomenon of day and night?

Day 3

Read: Ecclesiastes 3:11

He has made everything beautiful in its time. Also He has put eternity in their hearts, except that no one can find out the work that God does from beginning to end.

Respond: We know the Hebrew word for *beautiful* in this verse is *kairos,* a Greek word meaning "perfect timing." How do you think perfect timing plays into God's story in the stars?

How do you think God putting "eternity in our hearts" relates to the stars and our compulsion to be *Looking Up*?

Day 4

Read: Proverbs 25:2

It is the glory of God to conceal a matter, but the glory of kings is to search out a matter.

Respond: Why do you think it's important to God that you search out what the scriptures mean?

How do you think God helps you build a relationship with Him through being a "king" and searching out the deeper meaning of His Word?

How are you searching out His heavenly story?

Day 5

Read: Matthew 5:18

> ***For assuredly, I say to you, till heaven and earth pass away, one jot or one tittle will by no means pass from the law till all is fulfilled.***

Respond: God's attribute of immutability means He doesn't change; He is utterly dependable (see James 1:17, Hebrews 6:17-18; Psalm 33:11). What do the signs in the firmament tell you about God's unchanging character?

We often get tired of reading the same story over and over. Jesus' story in the stars plays night after night, month after month, year after year throughout the millennia and God never gets tired of it. Why do you think He plays it over and over again without getting bored?

Do you get tired of seeing the same stars, constellations and "story" play out year after year above your head? Why or why not?

Day 6

Use the following space to write any thoughts God has put in your heart and mind about the things we have looked at in this session and during your Daily Follow-Up time this week. If you haven't done so already, make sure to read the assignment for the next session in *Looking Up.*

Session Three

Seeing God's Story in the Stars

Memory Verse:

The heavens declare the glory of God; and the firmament shows His handiwork. Day unto day utters speech, and night unto night reveals knowledge. There is no speech nor language where their voice is not heard.

—PSALM 19:1-3

In Chapter One of *Looking Up* Pastor Troy mentioned the important characteristic of pattern recognition we humans possess. "I think that the difference the Holy Spirit makes within us separates us from brute beasts. It also causes us to see the patterns instead of being confused by them. God can engage our primitive brains with supernatural understanding through prophetic pictures in the stars. He has been broadcasting His deepest truths through the things He created" (see page 30). Psalm 19 not only makes an amazing statement about our Creator, it also begs us to search out the details; to talk to one another during the day and to expect revealed knowledge during the night hours.

Looking Up reading assignment for this session:

- Chapter Two (pages 50-71). Continue to review and familiarize yourself with the Looking Up Prophetic Pictures in the Heavens Map.

Preparing and Discussing

[Invite one of the group to open your conversation in prayer, asking God to give each of you an understanding and revelation of what He is saying in His creation and in His Word.]

1. Now that we've all read the first two chapters of *Looking Up*, we've traveled through the full cycle of the 12 signs in the firmament. What have you learned so far that you didn't know before?

2. What is your overall opinion of God's story in the stars now that you've read through the basics of the story as a whole?

   How does it compare to what you know about what astrologers call the Zodiac?

3. Is there a chapter in the story–a sign–that especially speaks to you? If so, which one is it and why does it shine brightly in your mind? Explain in your own words how the three supporting constellations surrounding the sign help tell the story.

The Word and the Message of the Stars

The following Bible passage connects with the main themes of the assignment in *Looking Up*. In fact, Psalm 19 is a foundation for the entire *Looking Up* study.

Let's hear this passage read as we follow along, and we will include these verses in our conversation about the book.

Psalm 19:1-14

> ***[1] The heavens declare the glory of God; and the firmament shows His handiwork.***
>
> ***[2] Day unto day utters speech, and night unto night reveals knowledge.***
>
> ***[3] There is no speech nor language where their voice is not heard.***
>
> ***[4] Their line has gone out through all the earth, and their words to the end of the world. In them He has set a tabernacle for the sun,***
>
> ***[5] Which is like a bridegroom coming out of his chamber and rejoices like a strong man to run its race.***
>
> ***[6] Its rising is from one end of heaven, and its circuit to the other end; And there is nothing hidden from its heat.***
>
> ***[7] The law of the LORD is perfect, converting the soul; the testimony of the LORD is sure, making wise the simple;***
>
> ***[8] The statutes of the LORD are right, rejoicing the heart; the commandment of the LORD is pure, enlightening the eyes;***
>
> ***[9] The fear of the LORD is clean, enduring forever; the judgments of the LORD are true and righteous altogether.***

4. When the Word says the sun is *"like a bridegroom coming out of his chamber and rejoices like a strong man to run its race. Its rising is from one end of heaven, and its circuit to the other end,"* what natural phenomenon do you suppose this verse is talking about?

____

____

5. When the passage says there is *"nothing hidden from its heat,"* it is a reference to the word *passion.* In your own words, how do you see the passion of God for you personally, as well as believers throughout time, in this revelation of the Bible written in the heavens?

6. Pastor Troy points out that verse 2 reminds us the daylight hours are for speaking and interaction, while the nighttime is for learning or receiving knowledge. How does the psalmist's mention of the sun in verse 3 relate to the specific 12 constellations that summarize God's story in the heavens?

How do they serve as a "tabernacle"? (See pages 38-39.)

7. Verse 9 speaks about the fear of the Lord. Pastor Troy's definition of the "fear of the Lord" comes from Proverbs 8:13. It is "to love what God loves and hate what God hates." Thinking about the story in the stars where Jesus is the hero who pays the ultimate price for His people then returns to set them free and defeat our enemy once and for all time, how has this story changed the way you look at Jesus?

How has it changed the way you look at the night sky?

Study Notes

As has been mentioned before, there is an important difference between *heavens* and *firmament* as the terms are used throughout God's Word and particularly in Psalm 19:1. *Heavens* is the wide, general scope of creation or the vast reaches of space; *firmament* is made up of the unchanging, regular, repeating, sure aspects of God's creation. It is literally our view of the universe from planet Earth because God created the universe to be seen from our perspective. He is speaking to us and only us through these signs in the heavens!

Looking Up and Seeing

Let's explore the meaning of some of what we've just been reading in *Looking Up*, Chapter Two.

8. In discussing the universal outline for storytelling on page 52, what are the three components of every great story?

   How do we see these three distinct components in the greatest story ever told?

Why do you think God insists on telling His story every year?

9. Pages 56-67 take us on our first tour of the 12 signs God uses to outline His story to us. Open to the first sign (Virgo) and note the way each constellation will be introduced: the star schematic, sign number, expanded name, supporting cast constellations that clarify the story point, and a brief look at that "chapter" of the story. In what ways was God intentional about telling this heroic tale?

Jesus is many things to us—brother, healer, redeemer—the list is long. Had you even considered Him to be a superhero? Why or why not?

10. On page 69 there is a review of the 12 signs, highlighting how Jesus is the central figure and hero in the story. In your own words, recreate the story sign by sign.

Virgo

Libra

Scorpio

Sagittarius

Capricorn

Aquarius

Pisces

Aries

Taurus

Gemini

Cancer

Leo

Applying the Word in the Constellations

Let's get personal about the content of these chapters and the passages from God's Word we have been considering.

11. On page 68 of *Looking Up*, Pastor Troy mentions Isaiah 40:26. Read that verse again. What comes to mind when you consider the words *"He calls them each by name"*?

What comes to mind when you think about the words *"not one is missing"*?

Final Matters

A parting thought from Pastor Troy:

> Know this: the story in the heavens is all about God's great vengeance upon the thing that separated us from Him and His great love. It is the story of restoration for those of us who are His. *"For the wrath of God is revealed from heaven against all ungodliness and unrighteousness of men, who suppress the truth in unrighteousness"* (Romans 1:18). Jesus is portrayed in the heavens as the fixer of the problem and the answer to the dilemma. That is who He is and how He wants to be known. It's important to Him that we see Him this way.

[As the session winds down, encourage the group to prepare for the next session and be in prayer for each of the other group members.]

Here are some last-minute tasks as we conclude this session:

- *Looking Up* reading assignment for next week: Chapter Three (pages 73-96).
- Prayer requests from the group about the need to identify and overcome points of inertia in our lives.

Close in prayer.

Daily Follow-Up

Day 1

Read: Daniel 5:27

TEKEL: you have been weighed in the balances, and found wanting....

Respond: When reading this verse on page 41 under the sign of Libra, what revelation do you get about God's judgment? Contemplate how judgment is different from justice.

____

____

____

____

Day 2

Read: Psalm 19:1-3

The heavens declare the glory of God; and the firmament shows His handiwork. Day unto day utters speech, and night unto night reveals knowledge. There is no speech nor language where their voice is not heard.

Respond: What do these verses tell you about the character of God toward His people? Toward those who do not know Him?

____

____

____

____

Day 3

Read: Hebrews 12:2

Looking unto Jesus, the author and finisher of our faith, who for the joy that was set before Him endured the cross, despising the shame, and has sat down at the right hand of the throne of God.

Respond: According to this verse, what is Jesus' primary attitude as He sits right now at the right hand of the throne of God?

What's He thinking as He looks at you? (See also Philippians 1:6.)

Day 4

Read: Psalm 19:7-9

The law of the LORD is perfect, converting the soul; the testimony of the LORD is sure, making wise the simple; the statutes of the LORD are right, rejoicing the heart; the commandment of the LORD is pure, enlightening the eyes; the fear of the LORD is clean, enduring forever; the judgments of the LORD are true and righteous altogether.

Respond: The law, testimony, statutes, and commandments of the Lord bring the blessing of good things into our lives. In what ways have you discovered that the fear of the Lord and the judgments of the Lord are enduring parts of His relationship with you?

Day 5

Read: Revelation 2:26-28; 22:16

And he who overcomes, and keeps My works until the end, to him I will give power over the nations—"He shall rule them with a rod of iron; They shall be dashed to pieces like the potter's vessels"—as I also have received from My Father; and I will give him the morning star.

"I, Jesus, have sent My angel to testify to you these things in the churches. I am the Root and the Offspring of David, the Bright and Morning Star."

Respond: What does Jesus mean by offering the morning star and identifying Himself as that star?

How is He the morning star to you?

Day 6

Use the following space to write any thoughts God has put in your heart and mind about the things we have looked at in this session and during your Daily Follow-Up time this week.

If you haven't done so already, make sure to read the assignment for the next session in *Looking Up*.

Session Four

Looking Closely at Act One

Virgo—Libra—Scorpio—Sagittarius

LOOKING UP
LOOKING UP
LOOKING UP
LOOKING UP

Memory Verse:

Do you know the ordinances of the heavens?
Can you set their dominion over the earth?

—JOB 38:33

The book of Job ranks alongside the books of Moses as the oldest writings in the Old Testament. Yet in the context of this week's memory verse, God asks Job questions that assume people were already well acquainted with the signs in the heavens. Notice Job 38:31-32, *"Can you bind the cluster of the Pleiades, or loose the belt of Orion? Can you bring out Mazzaroth in its season? Or can you guide the Great Bear with its cubs?"* God used the unchanging nature of the firmament as part of His overwhelming case to Job that the appropriate attitude of man toward God is utter awe and humility before His majesty, creativity, and sovereignty.

Looking Up reading assignment for this session:

- Chapter Three (pages 73-96). Continue to review and refer to the Looking Up Prophetic Pictures in the Heavens Map as you read.

Preparing and Discussing

[Open the session by calling the group to prayer, asking the Holy Spirit to open eyes and hearts as the groups seeks to *Look Up* in these sessions.]

1. Now that we are several weeks into this study, how would you describe the revelation of *Looking Up* to friends and family?

2. What are the four signs, or chapters, in Act One of the story of Jesus in the heavens?

What are the nearby constellations that support the plot and story line in each of these signs? (pages 56-59)

3. As you were reading through the pages (73-93) for this session, can you point to one insight, revelation, or fact that God used to speak to you about God's character?

Do you see Him as a superior storyteller, a mind-blowing mathematician or a brilliant scientist?

The Word and the Message of the Stars

The following Bible passages connect with the main themes of the assignment in *Looking Up*. Let's hear them read as we follow along, and we will include these verses in our conversation about the book.

Virgo

MATTHEW 1:23

"Behold, the virgin shall be with child, and bear a Son, and they shall call His name Immanuel," which is translated, "God with us."

Libra

DANIEL 5:27

TEKEL: You have been weighed in the balances, and found wanting....

Scorpio

ROMANS 5:8

But God demonstrates His own love toward us, in that while we were still sinners, Christ died for us.

Leo

REVELATION 6:2

And I looked, and behold, a white horse. He who sat on it had a bow; and a crown was given to him, and he went out conquering and to conquer.

4. The verses we just read relate to each of the signs for this week, as noted. In your own words, go through them one by one and describe the connection you find between the statement in the Word and the message in each sign.

___

___

___

5. Pastor Troy has already shared a little about why we begin with Virgo rather than the current assumption that the Zodiac should begin with Aries

(see pages 36-37). Why does it make more logical sense to start with Virgo than any other of the 11 constellations?

Do you agree with Pastor Troy's revelation that the Spinx is an astral structure that tells us where the story begins and ends? Why or why not?

6. Look at each of the four signs, Virgo, Libra, Scorpio and Sagittarius again and describe what each says about God and what each says about us?

7. Back on pages 45-47, Pastor Troy gave our first overview of the three acts which represent the progressive nature of the story in the heavenly signs. What part of the grand story of our salvation is covered in these first four constellations: Virgo, Libra, Scorpio, and Sagittarius?

What other Bible verses can you find that support or speak into your answer above?

Study Notes

Job 38, the source of this lesson's memory verse has an astronomy section following verses 4-30, which are about earth sciences and God's sovereignty over the world. Then verses 31-33 leap into the heavens. The three specific constellations mentioned (Pleiades, Orion, and Ursa Major) are all supporting constellations of the main 12-sign story line. Also, the term *Mazzaroth* in verse 32 is used in this section. Note the clue in the verse: *"Can you bring out Mazzaroth in its season?"* (Job 38:32a). The story in the stars is told through the seasons as set in place by God. We are not able to command or change their order, or speed their appearance. They are, as has been said, firmly positioned in the firmament.

Answer for question 11: John 1:14, Romans 9:5, Philippians 2:5-11, 1 Timothy 2:5, Hebrews 2:14.

Looking Up and Seeing

Let's explore together the meaning today of some of what we've just been saying.

8. Pages 75-80 focus on Virgo the Virgin and its brightest star, Spica. How do the meanings of the names for Spica relate to the identity and role of the child who will be born of the virgin?

______

______

______

What is it about the nature and ministry of Jesus that required He not only be born of a woman, but that the woman must also be a virgin?

______

______

______

9. Referring to the section on Libra the Scales (pages 81-85), Pastor Troy described the process of redemption written in the stars and confirmed in God's Word. Based on what you read, what does God mean when He announces in this sign, "You need redemption"?

How do the three supporting constellations near Libra (see page 57) confirm our need for a redeemer?

10. In the section on Scorpio the Scorpion (pages 86-90), what is the surprising truth about the way Jesus wars with death (1 Corinthians 15:55)?

Is there a difference between Jesus defeating sin and Jesus defeating death?

How is this conflict described in Genesis 3:15?

11. The fourth sign in this first act of the grand story of salvation is Sagittarius the Archer (pages 91-95). What was this Greek picture of this sign as half man/half horse revealing about Jesus?

Why is it crucial that the Son of God was also fully human?

As you review the Bible passages listed on page 93 that demonstrate Jesus was fully God AND fully man, which passages are in both lists? (There are five. See the Study Notes for the answer). For example, how does Philippians 2:5-11 show us the awesome glory of Jesus?

Applying the Word in the Constellations

Let's get personal about the content of these pages and the passages from God's Word we have been considering.

12. Read Luke 17:5-10. If someone said to you, "I get that Libra displays a grand set of scales and I even agree that my sin tips the scale badly against me. But why can't I just stack my good works and effort on the other side of the scales and balance them out," how would you answer that person?

Even if we did pile up some good works, when we try to put them on the scale, would they counterbalance our sin/works?

How did Jesus settle this in Luke 17?

---

13. The star Antares in Scorpio introduces the discussion of the number 16 on pages 88-89. What does the number 16 represent in Scripture?

As you read down the 16 descriptive names or "faces" of God in Scripture, which one(s) mean the most to you at this time in your Christian life?

Final Matters

A parting thought from Pastor Troy:

Reviewing this first act of the Salvation Story, in the first sign (Virgo), we learn the Messiah will be the seed of a virgin woman, fully God and fully human. In the second sign (Libra), we learn that the Messiah is just. He will pay the ransom for many and will pay the price only a divine Redeemer can. In the third sign (Scorpio), we find out the Messiah will be a mighty warrior who will confront and slap death in the face for all of us! He will defeat the dragon by going into the jaws of the dragon itself. Jesus will win the war over death by dying! And in the fourth sign, the Messiah is prophesied as an archer and a man of great warfare who is not afraid to deal with the enormous problem of the scorpion (death)—His arrow is pointed directly at the heart of the scorpion. He is strong, full of grace, and dual natured. This is the King of Kings as seen in Revelation, coming to conquer death. He is worthy of our worship and obedience!

[As the session winds down, encourage the group to prepare for the next session and be in prayer for each of the other group members.]

Here are some last-minute tasks as we conclude this session:

- *Looking Up* reading assignment for next week: Chapter Three (pages 97-115).
- Prayer requests from the group about the need to identify and overcome points of inertia in our lives.

Close in prayer.

Daily Follow-Up

Day 1

Read: Matthew 1:23

> ***"Behold, the virgin shall be with child, and bear a Son, and they shall call His name Immanuel," which is translated, "God with us."***

Respond: When you are praying, do you tend to assume your prayers have to travel to God—to His throne room—or do you sense that God is actually with you, willing to listen to your words and your heart?

How does your picture of prayer affect your willingness to pray?

Day 2

Read: Job 38:33

Do you know the ordinances of the heavens? Can you set their dominion over the earth?

Respond: Isn't it amazing that though everything in the universe is in motion, it is also following a plan fixed in the firmament by God?

How does the unchanging nature of God's plans and God's workmanship provoke you to trust Him more? Take a few moments to work on memorizing this verse.

Day 3

Read: Daniel 5:27

TEKEL: You have been weighed in the balances, and found wanting.

Respond: Since you are neither earning God's forgiveness nor repaying His redemption by the way you live, what is your motivation for living the Christian life?

Day 4

Read: Romans 5:8

> ***But God demonstrates His own love toward us, in that while we were still sinners, Christ died for us.***

Respond: In what ways have you experienced God as the great initiator in your relationship with Him?

What does this verse tell us about our need to fix ourselves or clean ourselves up before we come to Jesus?

Day 5

Read: Revelation 6:2

> ***And I looked, and behold, a white horse. He who sat on it had a bow; and a crown was given to him, and he went out conquering and to conquer.***

Respond: Is there anything in your life right now preventing you from wholeheartedly praying, "Come quickly, Lord"?

If the Holy Spirit shows you there is something hindering you, will you trust Him right now and let it go?

Day 6

Use the following space to write any thoughts God has put in your heart and mind about the things we have looked at in this session and during your Daily Follow-Up time this week.

If you haven't done so already, make sure to read the assignment for the next session in *Looking Up*.

Session Five

Looking Closely at Act Two

Capricorn—Aquarius—Pisces—Aries

Memory Verse:

And Jesus came and spoke to them, saying, "All authority has been given to Me in heaven and on earth. Go therefore and make disciples of all the nations, baptizing them in the name of the Father and of the Son and of the Holy Spirit, teaching them to observe all things that I have commanded you; and lo, I am with you always, even to the end of the age." Amen.

—MATTHEW 28:18-20

The four signs that make up the middle of the twelve share a water theme that is unmistakable. When Jesus told His disciples how they were to be busy making disciples now that He was risen and about to depart, He included in that command the step of taking those who became disciples into the water, prophetically re-enacting His own death, burial, and resurrection. This is called baptism. Baptism is also a prophetic type or shadow of the Red Sea parting in Exodus. You take the bondage Pharaoh has enslaved you with into the water but come out the other side—not only without your chains, but without Pharaoh and his army chasing you down. This should motivate us to live our lives as part of the vast catch of fish that Jesus promised as the result. These prophetic acts were pictured in the heavens long before they were written in the Word.

Looking Up reading assignment for this session:

- Chapter Three (pages 97-115). Continue to review the Looking Up Prophetic Pictures in the Heavens Map and using it to decode the scriptures and teachings you find in the book.

Preparing and Discussing

[Open in prayer, thanking God for the reality of the four constellations in this session as a picture of the life you are all living: part of Christ's body, gifted by His Spirit, called to multiply, seeing the Lord make all things new by His power and authority.]

1. Without looking, recite/write in order the four constellations we studied in Act One.

As you have reflected this past week on the first act of the constellations, what has God's Spirit led you to consider and think about?

2. What are the four signs in Act Two?

What other nearby constellations help highlight each of these? (Pages 60-63 list the second four constellations with their supporting-actor constellations.)

Because of their internal similarities, what name is given to these four constellations as a group?

Starting with the experience of Noah, brainstorm other places in the Bible where water, the sea, or fish have been central to the events?

3. The witches and New Age mystics believe these signs signify the "age of Aquarius" or "understanding." Knowing what you now know about these signs and their meaning in God's story, are they correct in their assumption? Why or why not?

How would you describe the Age of Aquarius from God's perspective?

In your own words, what is the big takeaway from the four signs in this section?

The Word and the Message of the Stars

The following Bible passages connect with the main themes of the assignment in *Looking Up.* Let's hear them read as we follow along, and we will include these verses in our conversation about the book.

Capricorn

JOHN 17:20-23

I do not pray for these alone, but also for those who will believe in Me through their word; that they all may be one, as You, Father, are in Me, and I in You; that they also may be one in Us, that the world may believe that You sent Me. And the glory which You gave Me I have given them, that they may be one just as We are one: I in them, and You in Me; that they may be made perfect in one, and that the world may know that You have sent Me, and have loved them as You have loved Me.

Aquarius

ACTS 2:17

And it shall come to pass in the last days, says God, That I will pour out of My Spirit on all flesh; your sons and your daughters shall prophesy, Your young men shall see visions, Your old men shall dream dreams.

Pisces

GENESIS 22:17

Blessing I will bless you, and multiplying I will multiply your descendants as the stars of the heaven and as the sand which is on the seashore; and your descendants shall possess the gate of their enemies.

Aries

MATTHEW 28:18

And Jesus came and spoke to them, saying, "All authority has been given to Me in heaven and on earth."

4. From your reading of the true meaning of the sign Capricorn, how would you explain the connection between Jesus' words in John 17:20-23 about the internal and eternal connection that exists between you and God Almighty?

____

____

____

How is Capricorn the Goat-Fish a picture of that relationship?

____

____

____

Where in this prayer does Jesus mention you?

____

____

____

5. It turns out that the lyrics "This is the dawning of the age of Aquarius" became a popular song by The 5th Dimension about 2,000 years too late. The Apostle Peter was actually quoting the Old Testament prophet Joel in Acts 2:17. Look up Joel 2:28-32 and discuss how much of Joel's prophecy has already come true in the Church and what part is still to come.

____

____

____

Do you feel this pouring out will be before the Rapture of the Church or during the Tribulation period? Why?

Aquarius is "pouring" out the Holy Spirit upon mankind. In what ways does that prophetic picture speak to you?

6. Stars, sand, and fish all serve as reminders of God's abundant provision. How does Pastor Troy explain the two fish tied at their tails that make up Pisces (pages 105-106)? What does the unchanging nature of the constellations in the firmament tell us about the character of our covenant-making God?

Historically, how has the picture of Pisces come to pass in the pages of the Bible?

How does the sign of Pisces fit into the books of Daniel, Revelation and end-times prophecy?

7. At what point in the story did Jesus tell His disciples, *"All power is given unto me in heaven and in earth"*?

Why is it crucial to realize this announcement occurred after He took His place as the perfect Passover lamb?

Notice the description on page 112 of the parallel between the Egyptian pagan honoring of Aries and God's instructions to His people regarding the Passover meal that would begin the Exodus. How does this fit with the fact that every one of the nine previous plagues or disasters that fell on Egypt made a mockery of one of their false gods?

Study Notes

Pastor Troy frequently mentions the work of E.W. Bullinger and his book *Witness of the Stars* (Kregel Publications, Grand Rapids, 1967). In that book, Bullinger outlines the three acts of the constellations as three books. Of this middle one he wrote:

> This Second Book began with the Goat dying in sacrifice, as it ends with the Lamb living again, "as it had been slain." The goat had the tail of a fish, indicating that his death was for a *multitude*

of the redeemed. In the two middle signs, we have had these fishes presented to us in grace and in their conflict. We come now to the last chapter of the book: and, as we have seen, like each of the other books, it ends up with victory and triumph. Here we are first shown the foundation of which victory rests, namely, Atonement. Hence we are taken back and reminded of the "blood of the Lamb."

Looking Up and Seeing

Let's explore together the meaning today of some of what we've just been saying.

8. In his brief description of the sign Capricorn on page 60, Pastor Troy pointed to the shift from the story of the great Redeemer who occupies the first four constellations to the story of the Redeemed, while never losing sight of the Redeemer. How does this sign highlight the prophetic picture of the phrase "Body of Christ"?

Why are both statements: 1) my relationship with Jesus and 2) our relationship with Jesus, essential parts our identity in Christ?

9. Review what Jesus said to the Samaritan woman of Sychar in John 4:13-14 and 21-24. How are Jesus' promises made true in the meaning of Aquarius?

What does it mean to you to worship God in Spirit and in Truth?

10. Twice in Jesus' training of the disciples He provided a miraculous catch of fish (Luke 5:1-11 and John 21:1-14). How are these events a prophetic picture of Pisces?

One catch was at the beginning of His ministry on earth, the other at the end. What do you think of the timing of these two events?

What was Jesus telling His disciples through these amazing catches about their purpose and destiny?

What is He telling you about your purpose and assignment?

11. On pages 113-114, Pastor Troy points to the significance of the 66 stars that make up Aries. How does this constellation point to one particular and unique Lamb?

In the prophetic picture of Aries, what is the Lord speaking into your heart and mind?

Applying the Word in the Constellations

Let's get personal about the content of these chapters and the passages from God's Word we have been considering.

12. If the first four constellations we studied reveal the identity of the Redeemer and these second four reveal the work of the Redeemer, how do you now better understand the opening words of Psalm 19, *"The heavens declare the glory of God; and the firmament shows His handiwork"*?

What have you heard of God's glory and what have you seen of His handiwork so far in this study?

13. One of the other books and studies from Pastor Troy's ministry is called *Redeeming Your Timeline,* in which he examines the truth that even the past, which we think is unchangeable, is not closed to Jesus. The key prophetic promise connected with Aries is Jesus' power and authority to make all things new—past, present, future. How have you experienced His power and authority on your past? Your present?

Final Matters

A parting thought from Pastor Troy:

> I have already stated that the story begins at Virgo (Genesis 3) and ends with Leo (Revelation 21). This is in accordance to the sequence of Revelation, and matches the Sphinx (head of a woman, body of a lion) that gives us an ancient and giant pointer to the exact place in the circle of the signs where the story begins. This is totally different from how the rest of the world views the Zodiac. Astrologers begin at Aries and end with Pisces because Spring starts in Aries. The bottom line here is, they have the facts, but they do not have the revelation. Why? The plan of redemption is hidden from idol worshippers, or idolaters. They have neither the revealed Word nor the revealing Spirit to guide them. They may see the stars, but they are actually lost in the dark.

[As the session winds down, encourage the group to prepare for the next session and be in prayer for each of the other group members.]

Here are some last-minute tasks as we conclude this session:

- *Looking Up* reading assignment for next week: Chapter Three (pages 116-135).
- Prayer requests from the group about the need to identify times and situations when we are failing to Look Up.

Close in prayer.

Daily Follow-Up

Day 1

Read: Mark 10:45

For even the Son of Man did not come to be served, but to serve, and to give His life a ransom for many.

Respond: You may have realized a long time ago you were one of the "many" Jesus was referring to in this verse. But how many people in your life are also among the "many" and they don't know it yet? As the Holy Spirit brings their names and faces to your mind, pray for them and ask for an opportunity to testify or share the gospel.

____

____

____

Day 2

Read: Matthew 28:18-20

And Jesus came and spoke to them, saying, "All authority has been given to Me in heaven and on earth. Go therefore and make disciples of all the nations, baptizing them in the name of the Father and of the Son and of the Holy Spirit, teaching them to observe all things that I have commanded you; and lo, I am with you always, even to the end of the age." Amen.

Respond: Jesus promised to be with you always. In what ways have you noticed His presence today? How have you responded to His faithfulness?

Day 3

Read: John 4:13-14

> ***Jesus answered and said to her, "Whoever drinks of this water will thirst again, but whoever drinks of the water that I shall give him will never thirst. But the water that I shall give him will become in him a fountain of water springing up into everlasting life."***

Respond: Would the people in your life say the fountain Christ has placed in you is springing up or would they note it seems clogged up? What can improve that situation?

Day 4

Read: Revelation 7:9

> ***After these things I looked, and behold, a great multitude which no one could number, of all nations, tribes, peoples, and tongues, standing before the throne and before the Lamb, clothed with white robes, with palm branches in their hands....***

Respond: In your Christian life so far, what's the closest you have come to experiencing some of what John was describing in this verse?

Day 5

Read: Revelation 21:5

Then He who sat on the throne said, "Behold, I make all things new." And He said to me, "Write, for these words are true and faithful."

Respond: Write out below at least five things you know Jesus has made new since you began to follow Him.

Day 6

Use the following space to write any thoughts God has put in your heart and mind about the things we have looked at in this session and during your Daily Follow-Up time this week.

If you haven't done so already, make sure to read the assignment for the next session in *Looking Up*.

Session Six

Looking Closely at Act Three

Taurus—Gemini—Cancer—Leo

Memory Verse

He has delivered us from the power of darkness and conveyed us into the kingdom of the Son of His love, in whom we have redemption through His blood, the forgiveness of sins.

—COLOSSIANS 1:13-14

The third act of the plan of redemption lies ahead of us. Because the first two acts in the drama have demonstrated God's faithfulness up until now, we have every reason to be confident in the future. God's Word never tires of restating, clarifying, and creatively describing the message He first declared in the stars. As Colossians 1:13-14 tells us, before we were made citizens of God's Kingdom, we were citizens of the kingdom of darkness. In Christ, we have a new citizenship in His Kingdom and expect to see our completed redemption through His blood. It's written in the firmament for those who will read it.

Looking Up reading assignment for this session:

- Chapter Three (pages 116-135). Continue to review the Looking Up Prophetic Pictures in the Heavens Map.

Preparing and Discussing

[Open the session in prayer, thanking the Lord once again for all He has done to make Himself known to us.]

1. We now have six weeks of memory verses to help us remember the lessons of *Looking Up*. Let's turn to pages 237-238 and read through them together. Which of these memory verses has become more precious to you and why?

2. What are the names and visual figures for the four signs in Act Three? What other nearby constellations help highlight each of these? (Pages 64-67 list the final four signs with their supporting-actor constellations.)

3. Now that we know the figures connected to each of the constellations, which one do you find most interesting? Why?

The Word and the Message of the Stars

The following Bible passages connect with the main themes of the assignment in *Looking Up*. Let's hear them read as we follow along, and we will include these verses in our conversation about the book.

Taurus

JOEL 2:11

The LORD gives voice before His army, for His camp is very great; for strong is the One who executes His word. For the day of the LORD is great and very terrible; who can endure it?

Gemini

2 CORINTHIANS 5:20-21

Now then, we are ambassadors for Christ, as though God were pleading through us: we implore you on Christ's behalf, be reconciled to God. For He made Him who knew no sin to be sin for us, that we might become the righteousness of God in Him.

Cancer

JOHN 10:28

And I give them eternal life, and they shall never perish; neither shall anyone snatch them out of My hand.

Leo

REVELATION 5:5

But one of the elders said to me, "Do not weep. Behold, the Lion of the tribe of Judah, the Root of David, has prevailed to open the scroll and to loose its seven seals."

4. Why does Pastor Troy begin his description of Taurus by saying, "Everything changes again at this constellation" (page 116)?

Which star in Taurus means "leader" or "governor"?

What is this star a prophetic picture of?

What do you think the Word means when it asks, *"Who can endure it"*?

5. Pastor Troy uses 1 John 3:2 (page 123) to demonstrate a main prophetic point about Gemini? What point is that?

What are the three brightest stars in Gemini and how do they uphold or enhance the story of Jesus in the heavens?

6. What part of John 10:28 gives you the most hope and comfort?

What negative thoughts or meanings does the word *cancer* already have?

What is the true meaning of the sign of Cancer in the stars?

Why is a crab offensive in Jewish culture?

What is the most important part of the crab sign and how is it connected to our modern medical community?

7. After the powerful signs in Taurus, Gemini, and Cancer, how does Leo complete the picture of Jesus as conquering King of kings and Lord of lords?

How and why is Leo connected to the tribe of Judah in Israel?

What is the significance of the elder's statement to John recorded in Revelation 5:5?

How is Jesus as the Lion of the Tribe of Judah different from the enemy in 1 Peter 5:8 who "prowls around like a roaring lion, seeking someone to devour"?

Study Notes

By this point in the study, you have been through three or four "cycles" of the twelve signs. You should be able to remember them in sequence, with a brief connecting description of each one and its part of the overall story. Can you tell the whole story?

Advances in astronomy have opened the eyes of man to the breadth and depth of space and the wonders it holds, yet the lie of the Zodiac has clouded our thinking. As a large portion of humanity wanders under the lies and distortions of astrology, giving the signs in the heavens god-like authority to guide their lives, we now know the truth hidden in plain sight above us.

Looking Up and Seeing

Let's explore together the meaning today of some of what we've just been saying.

8. Starting at page 75, let's look at each sign description and read the prophetic promise attached to each sign. What promises does God make throughout the story?

[Have everyone take out their Looking Up Prophetic Pictures in the Heavens Map and open it to the "red" side. Beginning with Virgo (on the back side) and moving through the signs, take turns reading the Prophetic Number section for each sign. Discuss how these numeric insights help you see the glory of God declared in the heavenly storybook.

9. Now read the Prophetic Promises for each sign. How do you see each of them play out in your life?

Applying the Word in the Constellations

Let's get personal about the content of these chapters and the passages from God's Word we have been considering.

10. Early in *Looking Up* (page 20), Pastor Troy wrote, "Another amazing thing about God is His extreme confidence in the hearts of humans. . . . So He took on the unimaginable challenge of communicating His message to every tribe, every race, every language, in every location throughout every time frame. And He did it. He did it first by writing it in picture, name and number form throughout the heavens." How do you see the signs in the night sky now that you have spent these weeks *Looking Up*?

11. Each sign in *Looking Up* has included a Star Party section that highlighted special stars within each sign. The next several sessions will focus on those stars and others, but what stars that you have read about so far have made an impression, and why?

Final Matters

A parting thought from Pastor Troy:

So you understand how the story ends. The good guy wins and He wins big! Jesus the Messiah will put down and shamefully destroy all works of darkness. Paul put it this way:

Then comes the end, when He delivers the kingdom to God the Father, when He puts an end to all rule and all authority and power. For He must reign till He has put all enemies under His feet. The last enemy that will be destroyed is death. For "He has put all things under His feet." But when He says, "all things are put under Him," it is evident that He who put all things under Him is excepted.

—1 CORINTHIANS 15:24-27

[As the session winds down, encourage the group to prepare for the next session and be in prayer for each of the other group members.]

Here are some last-minute tasks as we conclude this session:

- *Looking Up* reading assignment for next week: Chapter Four (pages 137-150).
- Familiarize yourself again with the blue side of the Looking Up Prophetic Pictures in the Heavens Map, noting the role stars and other heavenly bodies play in the constellations and throughout the heavens to declare God's glory.
- Prayer requests from the group about the need to identify and overcome points of inertia in our lives.

Close in prayer.

Daily Follow-Up

Day 1

Read: Joel 2:11

The LORD gives voice before His army, for his camp is very great; for strong is the One who executes His word. For the day of the LORD is great and very terrible; who can endure it?

Respond: In what ways is the fear of the Lord a good thing in your life as a follower of Jesus?

Day 2

Read: Colossians 1:13-14

He has delivered us from the power of darkness and conveyed us into the kingdom of the Son of His love, in whom we have redemption through His blood, the forgiveness of sins.

Respond: List at least three differences between your life as a citizen of Jesus' Kingdom and your previous life as a citizen of the kingdom of darkness.

Day 3

Read: 2 Corinthians 5:20-21

Now then, we are ambassadors for Christ, as though God were pleading through us: we implore you on Christ's behalf, be reconciled to God. For He made Him who knew no sin to be sin for us, that we might become the righteousness of God in Him.

Respond: What does it mean to be an ambassador of Christ?

Day 4

Read: John 10:28

And I give them eternal life, and they shall never perish; neither shall anyone snatch them out of My hand.

Respond: Describe how it affects your attitudes, outlook, and worldview to see yourself safely held in Jesus' hand?

Day 5

Read: Revelation 5:5

But one of the elders said to me, "Do not weep. Behold, the Lion of the tribe of Judah, the Root of David, has prevailed to open the scroll and to loose its seven seals."

Respond: We may find ourselves weeping for the lost today, but what will be the difference when the sign of Leo is fulfilled and Jesus comes to wipe away our tears and make all things right and new?

Day 6

Use the following space to write any thoughts God has put in your heart and mind about the things we have looked at in this session and during your Daily Follow-Up time this week.

If you haven't done so already, make sure to read the assignment for the next session in *Looking Up.*

Session Seven

God's Voice in the Stars (Part 1)

Memory Verse:

Those who are wise shall shine like the brightness of the firmament,
And those who turn many to righteousness like the stars forever and ever.

—DANIEL 12:3

Our next three reading assignments and sessions will take us out into the stars. The 12 signs (remember, they are the constellations the sun goes through) will still be on our radar–or in sight–but now we will look closely at the messages that can be unlocked from the sizes, distances, and relationships between the stars themselves that make up the signs. What we have discovered in the firmament of the signs will be confirmed by what we can observe among the stars. Daniel, who spent much of his life hanging out with the stargazers, or Magi, of Persia, noted that godly wisdom is constant just like we see in God's firmament. You're going to love this!

Looking Up reading assignment for this session:

- Chapter Four (pages 137-150).

Preparing and Discussing

[Open in prayer, asking God to further declare His glory and show His handiwork in the stars over the next several weeks of study.]

1. What adventures are you having as you talk to others about what you are studying in *Looking Up*?

____

____

____

2. What constellations and stars have you been able to identify on your own during this study? How have those discoveries affected you?

3. Which star or constellation name always makes you smile? Why do you think that is?

The Word and the Message of the Stars

The following Bible passages connect with the main themes of the assignment in *Looking Up*. Let's hear them read as we follow along, and we will include these verses in our conversation about the book.

ISAIAH 40:22

It is He who sits above the circle of the earth, and its inhabitants are like grasshoppers, who stretches out the heavens like a curtain, and spreads them out like a tent to dwell in.

REVELATION 4:2

Immediately I was in the Spirit; and behold, a throne set in heaven, and One sat on the throne.

HEBREWS 12:2

Looking unto Jesus, the author and finisher of our faith, who for the joy that was set before Him endured the cross, despising the shame, and has sat down at the right hand of the throne of God.

ACTS 13:47

For so the Lord has commanded us: "I have set you as a light to the Gentiles, that you should be for salvation to the ends of the earth.'"

4. Ancient people depended on unaided observation and revelation for their understanding of the heavens. They had not circumnavigated the globe and many believed the earth to be flat. What does that tell you about the revelation in Isaiah 40:22 that God "sits above the circle of the earth"?

How do prophetic pictures like "curtain" and "tent" offer an accurate idea of what the heavens appear like to us?

What do you think this verse says about God?

What scriptures speak to Jesus being the center?

To Him being the "way home" so you will never be lost?

That He is humble?

5. How does Hebrews 12:2 remind us that *Looking Up* is about a lot more than tilting our heads back at night to observe the skies?

Noting Polaris–the North Star–and its physical relationship to Ursa Major in the night sky, why is it a big deal that this verse says Jesus "sat down at the right hand of the throne of God"?

6. In Acts 13:47, Paul was preaching to Jews and Gentiles in Antioch (modern-day Turkey). He was quoting Isaiah 49:6 to reveal God's plan had always been to offer salvation through Israel to the rest of the world. What is the prophetic picture God painted in this verse?

How does that relate back to God's original promise and prophecy to Abraham that his offspring would be as the sands of the sea and the stars of the heavens?

Study Notes

As you review Pastor Troy's explanations of the significance of various stars, note how the placement, positions, names, brightness, associated numbers, and relation to other stars all hold possible insights and revelations about the Creator. Keep these possibilities in mind as you expand your exploration of the skies on your own.

Looking Up and Seeing

Let's explore together the meaning today of some of what we've just been saying.

7. In discussing the practical significance of Polaris, what was the point for the early settlers of the United States in traveling with Polaris always off their right shoulders?

   How was this different from the way escaping slaves used the North Star?

8. When Pastor Troy noted that Polaris is only the 50th brightest star, how did he use that fact to point out some significant qualities of Jesus Himself?

9. On pages 146-148, Pastor Troy highlights the significance of the seven bright stars in the Big Dipper. How does he explain the message about the Church of Jesus Christ found in the meaning of these stars?

10. How do the names of the seven stars (listed on page 148) help connect these bright points to the Church?

11. Look again at the bullets on page 150. What is the message the Big Dipper preaches?

Applying the Word in the Constellations

Let's get personal about the content of these chapters and the passages from God's Word we have been considering.

12. How has the revelation that Polaris, which represents our savior Jesus, is fixed in the night sky and all other heavenly bodies revolve around it changed the way you view the heavens? The way you view Jesus?

____

____

____

Why do you think God created the heavens to revolve around Polaris from our firmament?

____

____

____

13. On pages 149-150, Pastor Troy explored Job's experience with God mentioning the Big Dipper as He tested Job's capacity to handle the "why" questions of life. How do you think this study of the stars is helping you respond to "why" questions you face?

____

____

____

Final Matters

A parting thought from Pastor Troy:

The Big Dipper shows us what the seven stars, or the Church, is supposed to do. No matter how big or attractive we may be, our job is to point lost people to rescue and slaves to freedom. The Father pointed people to Jesus. The Holy Spirit points people to Jesus. John the Baptist pointed people to Jesus. The Bible points people to Jesus. The New Testament Christians pointed people to Jesus. Even Jesus pointed people to Himself: *"Then Jesus declared, 'I am the bread of life. He who comes to me will never go hungry, and he who believes in me will never be thirsty'"* (John 6:35).

[As the session winds down, encourage the group to prepare for the next session and be in prayer for each of the other group members.]

Here are some last-minute tasks as we conclude this session:

- *Looking Up* reading assignment for next week: Chapter Four (pages 150-161). Encourage everyone to continue the study and review process that the Daily Follow-up studies allow.
- Prayer requests from the group about the need to bring areas of wandering in our lives to the sure Polaris of Jesus.

Close in prayer.

Daily Follow-Up

Day 1

Read: Isaiah 40:22

It is He who sits above the circle of the earth, and its inhabitants are like grasshoppers, who stretches out the heavens like a curtain, and spreads them out like a tent to dwell in.

Respond: The next time (or the first time) you look at Ursa Major/The Big Dipper or Polaris/The North Star, take a few moments to thank Jesus for speaking to you and every generation through the heavens.

Day 2

Read: Daniel 12:3

Those who are wise shall shine like the brightness of the firmament, and those who turn many to righteousness like the stars forever and ever.

Respond: Now that you understand the meaning of firmament, what does it mean that wisdom *"shines like the brightness of the firmament"?* How can you use this revelation to turn many to righteousness?

Day 3

Read: Revelation 4:2

Immediately I was in the Spirit; and behold, a throne set in heaven, and One sat on the throne.

Respond: Ask the Holy Spirit to reveal to you what John was seeing when he wrote this verse.

What do you think the throne set in heaven looks like?

Day 4

Read: Hebrews 12:2

Looking unto Jesus, the author and finisher of our faith, who for the joy that was set before Him endured the cross, despising the shame, and has sat down at the right hand of the throne of God.

Respond: Now that you know the story of Jesus in the stars, what does it mean that He is the author and finisher of your faith or your life?

Day 5

Read: Acts 13:47

For so the Lord has commanded us: "I have set you as a light to the Gentiles, that you should be for salvation to the ends of the earth."

Respond: It was the Gentile nations of Greece and Rome who twisted God's story in the stars. They took the revelation of the Mazzaroth and sold it to the world as the "Zodiac." This tainted teaching is widely accepted and millions have gone–and will go to hell because of it. Looking at this verse, why do you think Pastor Troy chose it to speak of the Big Dipper?

Day 6

Use the following space to write any thoughts you have about the section you just studied. What revelation(s) stood out that made you go, "Wow!" or made you smile at the genius of God?

If you haven't done so already, make sure to read the assignment for the next session in *Looking Up*.

Session Eight

God's Voice in the Stars (Part 2)

Memory Verse:

Can you bind the cluster of the Pleiades, or loose the belt of Orion? Can you bring out Mazzaroth in its season? Or can you guide the Great Bear with its cubs? Do you know the ordinances of the heavens? Can you set their dominion over the earth?

—JOB 38:31-33

God asked Job dozens of questions in Job 38-41. Every one of them must be answered, "No," "Only You, Lord" or "Definitely not me." This book, perhaps the oldest in Scripture, dating back to the time of Abraham, includes God asking about specific items in the heavens and the firmament. These questions push us (as they did Job) to two important conclusions: First, God can do it all and does it all every day; second, we can do practically nothing other than *"repent in dust and ashes"* (Job 42:6). David had the same response in Psalm 8:3-4. All of our wonder over the heavens and discoveries about the firmament fall short of God's purpose if they don't bring us to humble worship before King Jesus.

Looking Up reading assignment for this session:

- Chapter Four (pages 150-161).

Preparing and Discussing

[Open in prayer, inviting God's manifest presence as you study what He has declared in the heavens and shown by His handiwork.]

1. Let's all open up our Looking Up Prophetic Pictures in the Heavens Map. What have you found most helpful about these summaries? In the top left-hand corner of the blue side, find the constellation Orion. It's not one of the 12 signs, but which of the 12 does it serve as a supporting actor? What

is the message in Orion and how does it speak of Jesus? (See page 64 in *Looking Up*.)

2. You've probably noticed that from our perspective, the constellations appear to be shining on a flat surface above us. However, we have discovered that no two stars in any constellation is the same distance from us—and some of those distances are mind-boggling. So, what is the significance of us being able to see them in the patterns that we do? What is God telling us by the way He lets us see the signs in the heavens?

3. What was your big revelation or "takeaway" from the section?

The Word and the Message of the Stars

The following Bible passages connect with the main themes of the assignment in *Looking Up*. Let's hear them read as we follow along, and we will include these verses in our conversation about the book.

JOHN 1:4-5

In Him was life, and the life was the light of men. And the light shines in the darkness, and the darkness did not comprehend it.

JOHN 9:5

As long as I am in the world, I am the light of the world.

REVELATION 2:16

Repent, or else I will come to you quickly and will fight against them with the sword of My mouth.

EPHESIANS 6:14

Stand therefore, having girded your waist with truth, having put on the breastplate of righteousness....

4. In the first verses of John 1, John creates a parallel with the creation account we read in Genesis 1. He's saying Jesus was there at creation, handling everything. What two things does this verse say Jesus provides for us as our Creator? Look at verse 9.

In light of the revelation of Jesus as the hero of the story in the heavens, how does the light (Jesus) shine in the darkness and in what ways does the darkness not comprehend it?

5. Read again what Jesus said in John 9:5. Since He has ascended to heaven and will return (hopefully any day now), how does the revelation of *Looking Up* prove that He is still the light of the world?

Although it is not a sign, the constellation Orion demands attention. Why do you think three of the brightest stars in our heavenly view are in this constellation? What are their names?

6. Who is speaking in Revelation 2:16? How does the prophetic picture in Orion speak of Jesus in this verse? Which star speaks of Jesus' imminent return? What facts did Pastor Troy point out about this star that support his premise?

7. In Ephesians 6, the Apostle Paul wants us to think of ourselves as spiritual warriors. What features of the constellation Orion echo Paul's list of spiritual equipment for battle? (See pages 157-159.) List the stars, meanings and numbers that support the prophetic picture of the full armor of God?

Study Notes

[If the group is intrigued by question 7, take a look at the longer passage, Ephesians 6:10-1,8 to discuss as a sign for spiritual warfare.]

Looking Up and Seeing

Let's explore together the meaning today of some of what we've just been saying.

8. Since this entire session is about Orion and his standout stars as the prophetic picture of Jesus, tell the story of Orion/Jesus in your own words as it is written in this constellation.

9. Pastor Troy highlighted the star Rigel. Explain the story line of Rigel. What facts about Rigel support Pastor Troy's premise about Orion as a picture of Jesus in the stars?

10. Read the quote on page 141 from professor Jim Kaler. What stars does he highlight and what part do they play in the drama of Orion?

    What do the numbers 5 (grace) and 17 (things unveiled in God's presence; Light of truth) related to Bellatrix say about Jesus?

11. Read quietly through the bullets on pages 159-160. In your own words, what is the amazing message Orion preaches?

Applying the Word in the Constellations

Let's get personal about the content of these chapters and the passages from God's Word we have been considering.

12. We began this session thinking about the humbling of Job. In what ways would you say you have been humbled during this *Looking Up* study?

____

____

____

13. The warrior aspect of Orion has brought up God's provision of spiritual weaponry and equipment for battle. From the list in Ephesians 6:10-18, which of those weapons might be gathering dust and rust in your spiritual life? What are you going to do about that?

____

____

____

Final Matters

A parting thought from Pastor Troy:

> I'm telling you, God will bless you if you start writing or singing about how Jesus is going to stomp out all of our enemies. And Paul had a revelation of who those enemies really are—not flesh and blood. A long time before John even had a revelation of it (Revelation 19:15), the heavens declared it through Orion and Rigel.

[As the session winds down, encourage the group to prepare for the next session and be in prayer for each of the other group members.]

Here are some last-minute tasks as we conclude this session:

- *Looking Up* reading assignment for next week: Chapter Four (pages 160-175).
- Prayer requests from the group about the need to identify and overcome points of inertia in our lives.

Close in prayer by turning to page 190 in *Looking Up* and praying Pastor Troy's "My Constellation Prayer." We will end each of the final three sessions this way.

Daily Follow-Up

Day 1

Read: John 1:4-5

In Him was life, and the life was the light of men. And the light shines in the darkness, and the darkness did not comprehend it.

Respond: Ask the Lord to show you in what ways Jesus is both life and light to you right now.

___

___

___

___

___

Day 2

Read: Job 38:31-33

Can you bind the cluster of the Pleiades, Or loose the belt of Orion? Can you bring Mazzaroth in its season? Or can you guide the Great Bear with its cubs? Do you know the ordinances of the heavens? Can you set their dominion over the earth?

Respond: How does it make you feel to realize that when you look up at the heavens you are doing the same thing Abraham, David and Jesus did? What does the fact that we don't look up much say about our attitude toward God?

Day 3

Read: John 9:5

> ***As long as I am in the world, I am the light of the world.***

Respond: Ask Jesus to reveal how He has been the Orion of your life. What did the Holy Spirit reveal to you?

Day 4

Read: Revelation 2:16

> ***Repent, or else I will come to you quickly and will fight against them with the sword of My mouth.***

Respond: When you read this passage and the rest of the letters Jesus wrote to the seven churches in Revelation, what do you think the "sword of his mouth" is speaking to the world? To you personally?

Day 5

Read: Ephesians 6:14

Stand therefore, having girded your waist with truth, having put on the breastplate of righteousness....

Respond: Meditate for a few minutes about what it actually means to "gird your waist with truth." How do you wear truth? Can others see that you are wearing truth?

Day 6

Use the following space to write any thoughts God has put in your heart and mind about the things we have looked at in this session and during your Daily Follow-Up time this week.

If you haven't done so already, make sure to read the assignment for the next session in *Looking Up*.

Session Nine

God's Voice in the Stars (Part 3)

Memory Verse:

Do all things without complaining and disputing, that you may become blameless and harmless, children of God without fault in the midst of a crooked and perverse generation, among whom you shine as lights in the world, holding fast the word of life, so that I may rejoice in the day of Christ that I have not run in vain or labored in vain.

—PHILIPPIANS 2:14-16

As we have seen in other passages, one of the ways God's Word highlights the purpose of the stars is to use them to inspire us to look for our personal identity, purpose and destiny. Here in Philippians 2, the Apostle Paul tells the believers that they are expected to *"shine as lights in the world, holding fast the word of life."* The word translated "lights" (phosteres) is a Greek word also used often for "stars." The word behind "world" is *kosmo*, which is connected to "cosmos," or universe. Paul was using the language of *Looking Up*! When we are *"holding fast the word of life,"* we are representing to a dying world the unchanging firmament of God's Word that offers life!

Looking Up reading assignment for this session:

- Chapter four (pages 160-175).

Preparing and Discussing

[Open with prayer, inviting participants to offer one sentence prayers of praise and worship to the Lord of the Universe, King Jesus.]

1. Looking at the 16 pages in this assignment, which star or heavenly body Pastor Troy highlights speaks to you most about Jesus? About your place in the cosmos?

2. What three shapes or figures do we see in Cassiopeia as that constellation appears to go around the North Star? In astronomical language this sign is one of the circumpolar constellations. According to Pastor Troy, what other constellation appears just at the point when Cassiopeia has turned right side up? What wonderful story does this change tell each night?

3. Talk about some examples of the number five and what it represents in God's dealings with us? What constellations or signs throughout *Looking Up* speak of the number 5?

The Word and the Message of the Stars

The following Bible passages connect with the main themes of the assignment in *Looking Up*. Let's hear them read as we follow along, and we will include these verses in our conversation about the book.

2 TIMOTHY 4:8

Finally, there is laid up for me the crown of righteousness, which the Lord, the righteous Judge, will give to me on that Day, and not to me only but also to all who have loved His appearing.

REVELATION 1:7

Behold, He is coming with clouds, and every eye will see Him, even they who pierced Him. And all the tribes of the earth will mourn because of Him. Even so, Amen.

EPHESIANS 2:8

For by grace you have been saved through faith, and that not of yourselves; it is the gift of God....

COLOSSIANS 2:6-7

As you have therefore received Christ Jesus the Lord, so walk in Him, rooted and built up in Him and established in the faith, as you have been taught, abounding in it with thanksgiving.

4. Cassiopeia's continual change from a W to a 3 to a M speaks to what aspects of our past, present, and future experience with Christ? How does Paul describe this process of salvation as previously sealed, immediately being worked out, and eternally "laid up" in 2 Timothy 4:8?

5. Revelation 1:7 speaks of every eye seeing Jesus at His return. Sirius is the brightest star in our view and is easily picked out of the sky night after night.

What does this say about Jesus' love for His people? Does it correspond or connect to Revelation 1:7? Why or why not?

6. What is grace as Paul uses it in Ephesians 2:8? Perhaps you've heard it spelled out as God's Riches At Christ's Expense. When Pastor Troy connects the number 5 with grace, he began with the example of salvationand added what other examples of God's riches? In what sense are the signs in the heavens and the firmament other examples of God's grace?

7. Read Colossians 2:6-7. How does the message in the Summer Triangle parallel this passage? How does it parallel the Gospel?

Study Notes

When Pastor Troy said at the beginning of *Looking Up* that the constellations near the 12 signs in the heavens, as well as the star names, distances, and magnitudes support the story, he was not joking. The message of the Gospel written in the stars is there for every man, woman and child throughout the Earth to see throughout all time. As you read this portion of the book, make note of the number of times the account written in the Bible parallels the story in the sky. Let it give you a deep appreciation for God Almighty as the greatest communicator ever. Let it sink in that the Creator of this vast, intricate account of His love for His creation includes the one reading these words right now. Consider the planning, precision, and purpose behind every detail in that starry canvas. How does it make you feel to know that it was written just for you? How does it make you feel to consider that you have taken the time to "search out the matter" (Proverbs 25:2)? God Almighty is speaking through the signs in the heavens and you have an ear to hear.

Looking Up and Seeing

Let's explore together the meaning today of some of what we've just been saying.

8. There's no doubt Jesus loves His bride–the Church–and is working to prepare her for eternity together. In your own words, how does the constellation Cassiopeia represent the bride of Christ in this prophetic picture?

____

____

____

9. On page 161, Pastor Troy says Sirius represents Jesus: the hope and ruler over the Gentile nations. How did Jesus actually fulfill this in His first coming to earth? How do you think He will fulfill this in the second coming at the end of the seven-year Tribulation?

____

____

____

10. What are the three stars in the Summer Triangle? How do their names and the numbers related to them tell the story of Jesus as found in the 12 signs of the heavens?

11. As it did in Chapter One of *Looking Up*, the number 12 again makes an appearance in Chapter Four. How does this number connect with the third sign in the summer triangle and what does it say about God?

Applying the Word in the Constellations

Let's get personal about the content of these chapters and the passages from God's Word we have been considering.

12. The number five plays a huge role in the Summer Triangle. In your own words, explain how the grace of five is found throughout this sign.

13. What is the message in the Summer Triangle? How does the "wild goose chase" fit the story?

Final Matters

A Parting Thought From Pastor Troy:

> Grace is the power to separate you for His use and call you holy. Grace is the God-given ability to not be afraid, but to walk in the spirit of power, love and a sound mind. I will take all He is willing to dish out! Pour it on me, Lord Jesus, and call me anointed! May that be the desire of your heart too.

[As the session winds down, encourage the group to prepare for the next session and be in prayer for each of the other group members.]

Here are some last-minute tasks as we conclude this session:

- *Looking Up* reading assignment for next week: Chapter Five (pages 177-188).
- Prayer requests from the group about the need to identify and overcome points of inertia in our lives.

Close in prayer by turning to page 190 in *Looking Up* and praying Pastor Troy's "My Constellation Prayer."

Daily Follow-Up

Day 1

Read: 2 Timothy 4:8

> ***Finally, there is laid up for me the crown of righteousness, which the Lord, the righteous Judge, will give to me on that Day, and not to me only but also to all who have loved His appearing.***

Respond: So, what's it like to know you have a crown of righteousness with your name on it waiting for you? What does Paul have in mind by the phrase *"all who have loved His appearing"?* How does that describe the message in the stars from this chapter?

Day 2

Read: Philippians 2:14-16

Do all things without complaining and disputing, that you may become blameless and harmless, children of God without fault in the midst of a crooked and perverse generation, among whom you shine as lights in the world, holding fast the word of life, so that I may rejoice in the day of Christ that I have not run in vain or labored in vain.

Respond: Notice the two attitudes that create a barrier to the kind of holy living God wants us to have: complaining and disputing. How can they keep you from shining as a light in the world?

Day 3

Read: Revelation 1:7

Behold, He is coming with clouds, and every eye will see Him, even they who pierced Him. And all the tribes of the earth will mourn because of Him. Even so, Amen.

Respond: Now that you've read *Looking Up* and understand the Gospel in the heavens, what does it mean to you that Jesus is *"coming on the clouds"?*

______

______

______

Day 4

Read: Ephesians 2:8

For by grace you have been saved through faith, and that not of yourselves; it is the gift of God....

Respond: From your perspective, what is the gift God put in the stars?

______

______

______

______

Day 5

Read: Colossians 2:6-7

As you have therefore received Christ Jesus the Lord, so walk in Him, rooted and built up in Him and established in the faith, as you have been taught, abounding in it with thanksgiving.

Respond: How does knowing the truth about the story of Jesus in the heavens make it easier to receive Christ into your life? Walk with Him? Be rooted or built up?

______

______

______

Day 6

Use the following space to write any thoughts God has put in your heart and mind about the things we have looked at in this session and during your Daily Follow-Up time this week.

If you haven't done so already, make sure to read the assignment for the next session in *Looking Up*.

Session Ten

Looking Up for Life

Memory Verse:

Now when these things begin to happen, look up and lift up your heads, because your redemption draws near.

—LUKE 21:28

Much of *Looking Up* has been a celebration of salvation. But salvation is just a part of the story. There are several chapters of the revelation of Jesus in the heavens that are playing out right now. We can have confidence that what started two thousand years ago with Virgo the Virgin will soon culminate with the coming of Leo the Lion of the Tribe of Judah to get His bride–a true happily *ever* after story. With the prophetic picture being played out before our eyes, we can be assured if there is a design, there is a designer. If there is a thought, there is a thinker. If there is a plan, there is a planner. This is why we should always be *Looking Up.*

Looking Up reading assignment for this session:

- Chapter Five (pages 177-188).

Preparing and Discussing

[Open in prayer, using the Overview section on the red side of the Looking Up Prophetic Pictures in the Heavens Map to thank God for showing us each of the messages of the 12 signs in the firmament.]

1. Let's have some closing stories and testimonies about how God has worked during these sessions in your own life and the lives of others.

2. Our reading for this session in *Looking Up* was all about conclusions; what conclusions have you come to while you have been learning to see into the heavens?

3. Tell us your favorite sign—not the astrological sign related to your birthday which is a pagan practice, but the sign in the firmament that speaks to you most about God's plan written in the stars—kind of like your favorite Bible verse.

The Word and the Message of the Stars

The following Bible passages connect with the main themes of the assignment in *Looking Up*. Let's hear them read as we follow along, and we will include these verses in our conversation about the book.

PSALM 8:3-4

When I consider Your heavens, the work of Your fingers, the moon and the stars, which You have ordained, what is man that You are mindful of him, and the son of man that You visit him?

PSALM 53:1

The fool has said in his heart, "There is no God."

MATTHEW 2:1-2

Now after Jesus was born in Bethlehem of Judea in the days of Herod the king, behold, wise men from the East came to Jerusalem, saying, "Where is He who has been born King of the Jews? For we have seen His star in the East and have come to worship Him."

LUKE 21:25

And there will be signs in the sun, in the moon, and in the stars; and on the earth distress of nations, with perplexity, the sea and the waves roaring....

4. Considering Psalm 8:3-4, imagine God's fingers creating and placing the stars and planets. What does it mean to you that He "ordained" them because He was being "mindful" of man?

5. The revelation of *Looking Up* and the story of Jesus in the heavens is the intersection between science and scripture. With this in mind, why is it foolish to claim there is no God?

6. Given that the people of Israel had spent a lot of time in the east as exiles, taking with them the Scriptures that tell about the God who rewards looking up, how do you think the wise men knew a king had been born who was worth worshipping?

7. In Luke 21:25, Jesus was predicting signs in the heavens as well as on earth. What have been some of the recent ones that confirm yet again that He could return any time?

Study Notes

Look up Isaiah 46:10 in your Bible. When you consider the stars and the story of redemption through a Savior it has proclaimed since before time began, do you better understand why it says God *"declares the end from the beginning, and from ancient times things that are not yet done"?* If there is a thought, there is a thinker, right? Speaking of this simple, yet powerful logic, consider the bombshell, "If there is a design, there is a designer." When it comes to a design or plan, Isaiah 46:10 drops the mic. Do you see it? *"Saying, 'My counsel shall stand, and I will do my pleasure,'"* is the Lord of all creation whispering, "I am outside of time. I told the story. I know the ending and it is good. You can trust Me with the little things because this gigantic drama over your head every night that rotates, prophesies, and testifies of Me—I made that and I Am Mighty to save you. I will do my pleasure and I am pleased with you!" He is, you know. He is so happy you picked up this book. He's so happy that you dove into this study and that you're going after decoding the nightly messages in His starry story with your Looking Up Prophetic Pictures in the Heavens Map. You can trust the Planner to fulfill the plan and it is GOOD!

Looking Up and Seeing

Let's explore together the meaning today of some of what we've just been saying.

8. Twice during this chapter you have read in large bold letters: IF THERE IS A DESIGN, THERE IS A DESIGNER! IF THERE IS A THOUGHT, THERE IS A THINKER! IF THERE IS A PLAN, THERE IS A PLANNER! How have you found this to be true in this study?

9. On page 182, Pastor Troy wrote, "When you are asked to believe that Jesus is Christ, you are not asked to check your brain at the door." How does this fit with Jesus telling us loving God takes all your mind as well as all your heart, soul, and strength (Mark 12:30)?

---

10. On pages 183-185, Pastor Troy talked about the prophetic anticipation of Jesus as well as the prophetic evidence He Himself offered about His identity. How has this overwhelming prophetic evidence in this study helped your faith increase?

---

11. How do you picture Leo the lion? C. S. Lewis went out of his way to present in his Narnia stories a lion who was scary and worthy of fear, yet you knew instinctively that He would protect you like no other. However, "he is not a tame lion." He is fierce with his enemies and fiercely loyal to His friends. So what does your Leo look like?

Applying the Word in the Constellations

Let's get personal about the content of these chapters and the passages from God's Word we have been considering.

12. What is your personal plan for continuing to explore the heavens? Have you found headlines about cosmic happenings that you can use the Looking Up Prophetic Pictures in the Heavens Map to decode what God is saying? Have you found someone knowledgeable who can help you look up in the night sky with more confidence?

13. The next time you hear someone say, *"The heavens declare the glory of God and the firmament shows His handiwork,"* how are you going to respond?

Final Matters

A parting thought from Pastor Troy:

> This very big plan is the intention of a very, very big God who puts you and me at a very high priority. The pictures in the heavens are meant to be viewed from our perspective. The things these signs represent, the names of the stars and the numbers associated with the science of astronomy, all share the same Kingdom themes! They all give evidence to those who will look up that the same Creator is behind it all. The message is clear, the plan is laid out and the Messiah is defined.
>
> I only want to believe what is true. I don't want to waste my time or my life dedicated to something that isn't a reality, and I stand in 100 percent confidence believing God loves me, knows me and has

redeemed me. I trust the Holy Spirit has used this study to help you reach that same confidence.

Here are some last-minute tasks as we conclude this session:

- If you haven't yet, consider arranging for a Star Party with the group in which you binge-watch the three recorded Star Parties by Pastor Troy that are readily available on YouTube.
- Prayer requests from the group about personal pursuit of further learning about the heavens and the firmament as well as about a next study for the group.

Close in prayer by turning to page 190 in *Looking Up* and praying Pastor Troy's "My Constellation Prayer."

Daily Follow-Up

Day 1

Read: Psalm 8:3-4

When I consider Your heavens, the work of Your fingers, the moon and the stars, which You have ordained, what is man that You are mindful of him, and the son of man that You visit him?

Respond: During these sessions, have you stopped stargazing and looking with more wonder and awe of God's creation? How has it changed your faith?

___

___

___

Day 2

Read: Luke 21:28

Now when these things begin to happen, look up and lift up your heads, because your redemption draws near.

Respond: Do words like *begin* and *near* mean we're now sure something is going to happen so we look up, or do they mean we keep looking up because one of these times it's going to happen? Are you seeing Bible prophecies come to pass?

Day 3

Read: Psalm 53:1

The fool has said in his heart, "There is no God."

Respond: If he is a fool for saying it in his heart, what does it make a man if he says "there is no God" out loud?

Day 4

Read: Matthew 2:1-2

Now after Jesus was born in Bethlehem of Judea in the days of Herod the king, behold, wise men from the East came to Jerusalem, saying, "Where is He who has been born King of the Jews? For we have seen His star in the East and have come to worship Him."

Respond: How has this *Looking Up* study given you greater insight into the story of the wise men coming to Bethlehem to worship Jesus? How has the Christmas narrative come into sharper focus for you?

Day 5

Read: Luke 21:25

And there will be signs in the sun, in the moon, and in the stars; and on the earth distress of nations, with perplexity, the sea and the waves roaring.

Respond: No matter what the headlines say, God's plan is still in motion. What do you need to train yourself to say when it looks like the verse above is coming true before your eyes?

Day 6

Use the following space to write any thoughts God has put in your heart and mind about the things we have looked at in this session and during your Daily Follow-Up time this week.

Small Group and Leader Helps

Resources to Make Your Small Group Experience Even Better!

Frequently Asked Questions about Small Groups

What do we do on the first night of our group?

Like all fun things in life—have a party! A "get to know you" coffee, dinner, or dessert is a great way to launch a new study. You may want to review the Group Agreement (pages 157-158) and share the names of a few friends you can invite to join you. But most importantly, have fun before your study time begins.

Where do we find new members for our group?

This can be challenging, especially for new groups that have only a few people or for existing groups that lose a few people along the way. We encourage you to pray with your group and then brainstorm a list of people from work, church, your neighborhood, your children's school, family, the gym, and so forth. Then have each group member invite several of the people on his or her list. Another good strategy is to ask church leaders to make an announcement or allow a bulletin insert.

No matter how you find members, it's vital that you stay on the lookout for new people to join your group. All groups tend to go through healthy attrition—the result of moves, releasing new leaders, ministry opportunities, and so forth—and if the group gets too small, it could be at risk of shutting down. If you and your group stay open, you'll be amazed at the people God sends your way. The next person just might become a friend for life. You never know!

How long will this group meet?

Most groups meet weekly for at least their first six weeks, but every other week can work as well. We strongly recommend that the group meet for the first six months on a weekly basis if at all possible. This allows for continuity, and if people miss a meeting they aren't gone for a whole month.

At the end of this study, each group member may decide if he or she wants to continue on for another study. Some groups launch relationships for years to come, and others are stepping-stones into another group experience. Either way, enjoy the journey.

Can we do this study on our own?

Absolutely! This may sound crazy, but one of the best ways to do this study is not with a full house but with a few friends. You may choose to gather with another couple who would enjoy some relational time (perhaps going to the movies or having a quiet dinner) and then walking through this study. Jesus will be with you even if there are only two of you (Matthew 18:20).

What if this group is not working for us?

You're not alone! This could be the result of a personality conflict, life stage difference, geographical distance, level of spiritual maturity, or any number of things. Relax. Pray for God's direction, and at the end of this ten-week study, decide whether to continue with this group or find another. You don't typically buy the first car you look at or marry the first person you date, and the same goes with a group. However, don't bail out before the ten weeks are up—God might have something to teach you. Also, don't run from conflict or prejudge people before you have given them a chance. God is still working in your life, too!

Who is the leader?

Most groups have an official leader. But ideally, the group will mature and members will rotate the leadership of meetings. We have discovered that healthy groups rotate hosts/leaders and homes on a regular basis. This model ensures that all members grow, give their unique contribution, and develop their gifts. This study guide and the Holy Spirit can keep things on track even when you rotate leaders. Christ has promised to be in your midst as you gather. Ultimately, God is your leader each step of the way.

How do we handle the childcare needs in our group?

Very carefully. Seriously, this can be a sensitive issue. We suggest that you empower the group to openly brainstorm solutions. You may try one option that works for a while and then adjust over time. Our favorite approach is for adults to meet in the living room or dining room and to share the cost of a babysitter (or two) who can watch the kids in a different part of the house. This way, parents don't have to be away from their children all evening when their children are too young to be left at home. A second option is to use one home for the kids and a second home (close by or a phone call away) for the adults. A third idea is to rotate the responsibility of providing a lesson or care for the children either in the same home or in another home nearby. This can be an incredible blessing for kids. Finally, the most common solution is to decide that you need to have a night to invest in your spiritual lives individually or as a couple and to make your own arrangements for childcare. No matter what decision the group makes, the best approach is to dialogue openly about both the problem and the solution.

LOOKING UP
LOOKING UP
LOOKING UP
LOOKING UP

Small Group Agreement

Our Purpose

To provide a predictable environment where participants experience authentic community and spiritual growth.

Our Values

Group Attendance

To give priority to the group meeting. We will call or email if we will be late or absent. (Completing the Group Calendar on page 161 will minimize this issue.)

Safe Environment

To help create a safe place where people can be heard and feel loved. (Please, no quick answers, snap judgments, or simple fixes.)

Respect Differences

To be gentle and gracious to fellow group members with different spiritual maturity, personal opinions, temperaments, or "imperfections." We are all works in progress.

Confidentiality

To keep anything that is shared strictly confidential and within the group, and to avoid sharing improper information about those outside the group.

Encouragement for Growth

To be not just takers but givers of life. We want to spiritually multiply our life by serving others with our God-given gifts.

Shared Ownership

To remember that every member is a minister and to ensure that each attender will share a small team role or responsibility over time.

Rotating Hosts/Leaders and Homes

To encourage different people to host the group in their homes and to rotate the responsibility of facilitating each meeting. (See the Group Calendar on page 161.)

Our Expectations

- Refreshments/mealtimes ______________________________
____
- Childcare______________________________________
____
- When we will meet (day of week) ________________________
- Where we will meet (place) ____________________________
- We will begin at (time) ____________ and end at ____________
- We will do our best to have some or all of us attend a worship service together. Our primary worship service time will be ____________________
- Date of this agreement ________________________________
- Date we will review this agreement again _____________________
- Who (other than the leader) will review this agreement at the end of this study
____

Group Calendar

Planning and calendaring can help ensure the greatest participation at every meeting. At the end of each meeting, review this calendar. Be sure to include a regular rotation of host homes and leaders, and don't forget birthdays, socials, church events, holidays, and mission/ministry projects.

Date	Lesson	Host Home	Dessert/Meal	Leader

Memory Verse Cards

Session One

Lift up your eyes on high, and see who has created these things, who brings out their host by number; He calls them all by name. By the greatness of His might and the strength of His power; not one is missing.

—ISAIAH 40:26

Session Two

Then God said, "Let there be lights in the firmament of the heavens to divide the day from the night; and let them be for signs and seasons, and for days and years."

—GENESIS 1:14

Session Three

The heavens declare the glory of God; and the firmament shows His handiwork. Day unto day utters speech, and night unto night reveals knowledge. There is no speech nor language where their voice is not heard.

—PSALM 19:1-3

Session Four

Do you know the ordinances of the heavens? Can you set their dominion over the earth?

—JOB 38:33

Session Five

To Him [Jesus Christ] *who loved us and washed us from our sins in His own blood, and has made us kings and priests to His God and Father, to Him be glory and dominion forever and ever. Amen.*

—REVELATION 1:5-6

Session Six

He has delivered us from the power of darkness and conveyed us into the kingdom of the Son of His love, in whom we have redemption through His blood, the forgiveness of sins.

—COLOSSIANS 1:13-14

Session Seven

Those who are wise shall shine like the brightness of the firmament, and those who turn many to righteousness like the stars forever and ever.

—DANIEL 12:3

Session Eight

Can you bind the cluster of the Pleiades, or loose the belt of Orion? Can you bring out Mazzaroth in its season? Or can you guide the Great Bear with its cubs? Do you know the ordinances of the heavens? Can you set their dominion over the earth?

—JOB 38:31-33

Session Nine

Do all things without complaining and disputing, that you may become blameless and harmless, children of God without fault in the midst of a crooked and perverse generation, among whom you shine as lights in the world, holding fast the word of life, so that I may rejoice in the day of Christ that I have not run in vain or labored in vain.

—PHILIPPIANS 2:14-16

Session Ten

Now when these things begin to happen, look up and lift up your heads, because your redemption draws near.

—LUKE 21:28

Prayer and Praise Report

SESSIONS ONE, TWO, AND THREE

Prayer Requests

Praise Requests

SESSIONS FOUR AND FIVE

Prayer Requests

Praise Requests

Sessions Six and Seven
Prayer Requests
Praise Requests

Sessions Eight, Nine, and Ten
Prayer Requests
Praise Requests

Small Group Roster

Name	Email	Phone #

Hosting an Open House

If you're starting a new group, try planning an "open house" before your first formal group meeting. Even if you have only two to four core members, it's a great way to break the ice and to consider prayerfully who else might be open to joining you over the next few weeks. You can also use this kick-off meeting to hand out study guides, spend some time getting to know each other, discuss each person's expectations for the group and briefly pray for each other. A simple meal or good desserts always make a kick-off meeting more fun.

After people introduce themselves and share how they ended up being at the meeting (you can play a game to see who has the wildest story!), have everyone respond to a few icebreaker questions:

- What is your favorite family vacation?
- What is one thing you love about your church/our community?
- What are three things about your life growing up that most people here don't know?

Next, ask everyone to tell what he or she hopes to get out of the study. You might want to review the Small Group Agreement and talk about each person's expectations and priorities.

Finally, set an open chair (maybe two) in the center of your group and explain that it represents someone who would enjoy or benefit from this group but who isn't here yet. Ask people to pray about inviting someone to join the group over the next few weeks. Hand out postcards and have everyone write an invitation or two. Don't worry about ending up with too many people; you can always have one discussion circle in the living room and another in the dining room. Each group could then report prayer requests and progress at the end of the session.

You can skip this kick-off meeting if your time is limited, but you'll experience a huge benefit if you take the time to connect with each other in this way.

Leading for the First Time

- **Sweaty palms are a healthy sign.** The Bible says God is gracious to the humble. Remember who is in control; the time to worry is when you're not worried. Those who are soft in heart (and sweaty palmed) are those whom God is sure to speak through.
- **Seek support.** Ask your leader, co-leader, or close friend to pray for you and prepare with you before the session. Walking through the study will help you anticipate potentially difficult questions and discussion topics.
- **Bring your uniqueness to the study.** Lean into who you are and how God wants you to uniquely lead the study.
- **Prepare. Prepare. Prepare.** Go through the session several times. Consider writing in a journal or fasting for a day to prepare yourself for what God wants to do. Don't wait until the last minute to prepare.
- **Ask for feedback so you can grow.** Perhaps in an email or on cards handed out at the study, have everyone write down three things you did well and one thing you could improve on. Don't get defensive. Instead, show an openness to learn and grow.
- **Prayerfully consider launching a new group.** This doesn't need to happen overnight, but God's heart is for this to take place over time. Not all Christians are called to be leaders or teachers, but we are all called to be "shepherds" of a few someday.
- **Share with your group what God is doing in your heart.** God is searching for those whose hearts are fully His. Share your trials and victories. We promise that people will relate.
- **Prayerfully consider whom you would like to pass the baton to next week.** It's only fair. God is ready for the next member of your group to go on the faith journey you just traveled. Make it fun, and expect God to do the rest.

LOOKING UP

LOOKING UP

LOOKING UP

LOOKING UP

Leadership Training 101

Congratulations! You have responded to the call to help shepherd Jesus' flock. There are few other tasks in the family of God that surpass the contribution you will be making. As you prepare to lead, whether it is one session or the entire series, here are a few thoughts to keep in mind. We encourage you to read these and review them with each new discussion leader before he or she leads.

1. Remember that you are not alone.

God knows everything about you, and He knew that you would be asked to lead your group. Remember that it is common for all good leaders to feel that they are not ready to lead. Moses, Solomon, Jeremiah and Timothy were all reluctant to lead. God promises, *"Never will I leave you; never will I forsake you"* (Hebrews 13:5). Whether you are leading for one evening, for several weeks, or for a lifetime, you will be blessed as you serve.

2. Don't try to do it alone.

Pray right now for God to help you build a healthy leadership team. If you can enlist a co-leader to help you lead the group, you will find your experience to be much richer. This is your chance to involve as many people as you can in building a healthy group. All you have to do is call and ask people to help. You'll probably be surprised at the response.

3. Just be yourself. If you won't be you, who will?

God wants you to use your unique gifts and temperament. Don't try to do things exactly like another leader; do them in a way that fits you! Just admit it when you don't have an answer, and apologize when you make a mistake. Your group will love you for it, and you'll sleep better at night!

4. Prepare for your meeting ahead of time.

Review the session and the leader's notes, and write down your responses to each question. Pay special attention to exercises that ask group members to do something other than engage in discussion. These exercises will help your group live what the Bible teaches, not just talk about it.

5. Pray for your group members by name.

Before you begin your session, go around the room in your mind and pray for each member by name. You may want to review the prayer list at least once a week. Ask God to use your time together to touch the heart of every person uniquely. Expect God to lead you to whomever He wants you to encourage or challenge in a special way. If you listen, God will surely lead!

6. When you ask a question, be patient.

Someone will eventually respond. Sometimes people need a moment or two of silence to think about the question. Keep in mind, if silence doesn't bother you, it won't bother anyone else. After someone responds, affirm the response with a simple "thanks" or "good job." Then ask, "How about somebody else?" or "Would someone who hasn't shared like to add anything?" Be sensitive to new people or reluctant members who aren't ready to say, pray or do anything. If you give them a safe setting, they will blossom over time.

7. Provide transitions between questions.

When guiding the discussion, always read aloud the transitional paragraphs and the questions. Ask the group if anyone would like to read the paragraph or Bible passage. Don't call on anyone, but ask for a volunteer, and then be patient until someone begins. Be sure to thank the person who reads aloud.

8. Break up into smaller groups each week or they won't stay.

If your group has more than seven people, we strongly encourage you to have the group gather sometimes in discussion circles of three or four people during the appropriate sections of the study. With a greater opportunity to talk in a small circle, people will connect more with the study, apply more quickly what they're learning and ultimately get more out of it. A small circle also encourages a quiet person to participate and tends to minimize the effects of a more vocal or dominant member. It can also help people feel more loved in your group. When you gather again at the end of the section, you can have one person summarize the highlights from each circle. Small circles are also helpful during prayer time. People who are unaccustomed to praying aloud will feel more comfortable trying it with just two or three others. Also, prayer requests won't take as much time, so circles will have more time to actually pray. When you gather back with the whole group, you can have one person from each circle briefly update everyone on the prayer requests. People are more willing to pray in small circles if they know that the whole group will hear all the prayer requests.

9. Rotate facilitators weekly.

At the end of each meeting, ask the group who should lead the following week. Let the group help select your weekly facilitator. You may be perfectly capable of leading each time, but you will help others grow in their faith and gifts if you give them opportunities to lead. You can use the Small Group Calendar to fill in the names of all meeting leaders at once if you prefer.

10. One final challenge (for new or first-time leaders):

Before your first opportunity to lead, look up each of the five passages listed below. Read each one as a devotional exercise to help yourself develop a shepherd's heart. Trust us on this one. If you do this, you will be more than ready for your first meeting.

- Matthew 9:36
- 1 Peter 5:2-4
- Psalm 23
- Ezekiel 34:11-16
- 1 Thessalonians 2:7-8, 11-12

NOTES